P9-DHT-217

The Beginner's Guide to the Internet

By

Patrick J. Suarez

©1995
The Hanford Press®
All rights reserved.
No part of this book may be reproduced in any way
without prior written permission by The Hanford Press®

North Canton, Ohio U.S.A.

Deluxe, hardcover edition—Copyright - 1995
The Hanford Press, North Canton, Ohio, in association with
Patrick J. Suarez/Suarez Associates, Springfield, Ohio (E-mail: pat@bgi.com)

All rights reserved. No part of this book may be reproduced in any form, or by any
means, without the written permission of the author.

The information in this book is subject to change without notice. The author makes no
warranty of any kind with regard to this material, including use of the software mentioned or described herein. While every precaution has been taken in the preparation of
this book, neither the author nor the publisher shall have any liability to any person or
entity with respect to any liability, loss, or damage caused or alleged to be caused
directly or indirectly by the instructions in this book or by the computer products
described herein.

All rights are reserved. This book and its contents are the intellectual property of
Patrick J. Suarez. This book contains information that is protected by copyright. No
part of this book may be copied, reproduced, or translated into another language without the prior written consent of the author.

There are several references to trade names throughout this book. They are identified
by capitalization. They are the property of and owned by their respective creators and
companies, and this is hereby formally acknowledged. Their presence is required to
enhance the educational process only.

ISBN 1-884889-09-3

Printed in the U. S.A.

This book is dedicated with love to my wonderful wife, Jeannie, and my two terrific sons, Greg and Justin, all of whom showed patience and support throughout a very long process. You are great companions in this roller-coaster experience we call life.

FORWARD

"A friend in the business..." Virtually everyone has wished they had a "friend in the business" at one time or another. Like when the plumbing backs up on a holiday, or when the instructions that came with a new electronic gizmo, promising to be simple enough for a three year old, only make sense if the three year old also had a degree in Electrical Engineering. In short, there are many times we need a friendly, helping hand from someone with specific expertise.

The world of computers is a jungle of electronic voo doo to many, otherwise normal, people. Brave, well educated, mentally healthy people shiver in terror, palms sweating at the thought of advancing beyond the game playing level of computer use. Those, however, lucky enough to know Pat Suarez, professionally or personally, have a true friend in the computer business!

Pat has a unique manner for putting complex concepts into easy to understand terms. His witty, insightful manner of speaking and writing has broadened his respect and popularity from a neighborhood to global level.

Those who have attended classes or seminars featuring Pat Suarez come away with the confidence that they have truly learned something about the subject at hand and had fun in the process! Pat's warm, entertaining manner gives students, on any level, the feeling that they are listening to or reading notes from a friend, a very talented friend!

In "THE BEGINNER'S GUIDE TO THE INTERNET," Pat Suarez has again taken a complex concept, new to many people, and has presented the material in simple English. The result is a book that is as much fun to read as it is informative.

As you approach this book, fasten your seat belt, the "Information Super Highway" is just ahead, and getting there is, indeed, half the fun!

Jack Oberleitner
Author, Lector

i

Preface

This book is divided into four main areas. Part 1 introduces the Internet newcomer to the basic concepts of communication that he or she should know. There is not much detail, and none was intended. The intention of Part 1 is to impart enough knowledge to make the reader as productive as possible in as short a time as possible.

That same spirit of not overwhelming those new to the Net but allowing them to become productive quickly carries over into Parts 2 and 3. Part 2 describes accessing the Internet more or less indirectly by using a computer and modem that essentially become a terminal on a bigger computer that has direct access to the Internet system. Part 3 explains how the reader can use his or her own computer not as a mere terminal but as a machine that has its own direct access to the Internet system.

The final section of the book, the appendices, offers auxiliary information to which the reader will refer from time to time as he or she explores more deeply into Internet tools.

Ultimately, the most comprehensive Internet knowledge will come from simply using its tools, beginning with electronic mail.

This book and its author had some impressive help before and during its creation, so here are people to thank wholeheartedly, and in no particular order.

Thanks to the multi-talented Jack Oberleitner for guiding me through the winding road of publishing, and for being a close friend with good advice. Brian Brumley, for creating a marvelous interface for *The Beginner's Guide to the Internet* for Windows, and for having the kind off-center sense of humor it took to load BGI/Win with some great graphics. To Rick Hazen for his wonderful BGI/Mac design and programming. It took a lot of time to find someone with Rick's Mac talent, but the wait was worth it. To my cousin, Ben Suarez, for publishing this work, and to his Hanford Press staff for enduring my many moods and prodding, and for getting the job done beautifully. To Leslie Fulford and Lisa Lasarenko at Computer Group Duplication Services for their terrific work in packaging my software and for having a unique blend of humor and professionalism. To Luke Gain, the patient Internet wizard who reviewed this volume and answered more questions than he expected. To Delphi's Walt Howe, an early, pleasant, and cheerful Internet mentor who also answered many questions patiently. And finally, to a fellow I've never met, but who did a public critique of the first version of BGI/DOS. His review was so thorough that he taught me many things I needed to learn, as well as accomplishing the kind of results normally reserved for the most stringent beta test. Albert Crosby, where ever you are, thanks!

TABLE OF CONTENTS

PART 1
Basics and Background

CHAPTER 1
THE INTERNET: YOUR WINDOW ON THE WORLD

When historians write about the last decade of the twentieth century, they will discuss the communications revolution that brought over 100 million people together, revolutionized shopping, and changed the way we work and play. From our present vantage point in the mid-1990's, we are watching this revolution happen, and the main vehicle is the **Internet,** that global interlinking of individual computers and computer networks.

But the Internet is not about computers. Rather, it is about people, personal and mass communication, and getting and giving information; computers are merely the vessels through which all of this passes. And, while the Internet is the physical medium, the inanimate driving force behind this revolution is our need and desire to make information more plentiful, and to make communication more rapid, widespread, productive, and immediate.

Coincidentally, we might also make these global resources easier to understand and use.

So, what exactly is the Internet? The Internet is a way to do two things:

• Communicate with people

• Retrieve information

Let's consider the Net from two aspects, first as hardware, then as software. As hardware, the Net is a global collection of four million computers we call **hosts,** computers that offer information and services to other computers. Signals travel to and from all these hosts, and eventually to you, through a maze of wires and fiber optic cable (and the occasional satellite). The wires usually are common copper telephone lines, but can be high quality copper cables capable of carrying signals at high rates of speed. Fiber optic lines move signals even more quickly.

We'll take a look at the transmission line system in a bit. For now, all you need to remember is that Internet traffic moves from host to host, usually over either copper wire or fiber optic cable.

As software, Internet productivity is achieved by programs that allow you to send and receive electronic mail, log into other networks, transfer computer files to and from host systems that store files, and share and capture useful (and sometimes trivial) data and information. Depending on how you connect to the Internet, these programs may be located on the host system which you access, by modem or network, for your Internet link to the world, on your own computer's hard drive.

We call these individual programs **client** software. Later, we will look at these programs, and the one, central program called TCP/IP which allows Internet hosts to communicate and pass traffic back and forth. You'll meet TCP/IP in Chapter 3.

Before we go any farther, you must be aware of a few things. First, there are very few absolutes regarding the Internet. From the number of users to what you can do with an Internet tool, many factors can intervene and make a condition valid in one case and invalid in another.

Second, the power of the Internet lies in what each host has to offer to other host systems. There could be no effective file sharing if nobody were willing to establish file servers. We could not expand our knowledge base at the speed of electricity if all network executives erected impenetrable barriers to their systems. We could not learn from each other's experiences if everyone stopped sending their thoughts and opinions in electronic mail messages.

Third, the Internet is dynamic. Each day, literally, brings changes in how and where you access something and every day is another day of growth and expansion. Growth. There is continuous growth. More hosts, more people, more files, more information. Every day.

Fourth, from its inception, the Internet was an evolving creature. It still is; it always will be. Methods of access today that people consider to be state-of-the-art will soon be yesterday's nostalgia. A year is an eternity where Internet technology is concerned.

Fifth, the Internet is no longer a non-commercial medium meant just for university professors, military strategists, and computer technophiles. It is a commercial entity in which you may, in fact, carry on marketing and commerce. The Internet is already affecting how we buy most everything from a to z.

Want to buy a compact disk, plan a trip, peruse a catalog, purchase a shirt, order some flowers, market your wares, or seal a deal? The Internet's resources will let you do all of this and more, in living color on your computer screen.

This is not to say that the Internet is no longer an educational resource. Far from it. In fact, the Internet is beginning to play a central role in redefining how we educate our children and how students perform research, learn to interact with the rest of the human race, and, when all is said and done, learn how to learn. Computers, global links, and books are the tools of the student of the future. Your sixth grader doesn't have her own Internet connection? She's already behind the learning curve.

Finally, this book is meant as a basic tool. It is not 1,000 pages long, nor is it the last word in Internet encyclopedia.

But, this book will teach you what you need to know to become productive as quickly as possible. And, despite what you've read in the newspaper, there is nothing difficult in grasping the tools of the Internet. Really. Over ten million people use the Internet every day. Some folks think that number might be as high as thirty million. Ten to thirty million people on the Net every day?

How hard could this be to learn? In truth, not very, if you learn each Internet tool, one at a time, starting with electronic mail and learn and use only as much as you need to at any given time, while filling in knowledge gaps, as required, later.

4

The intimidation facing Internet newcomers is the feeling that:

- there is so much to learn,

- they have to learn it all immediately,

- it's about computers, or at least a facet of computing with which they have almost no familiarity,

- Unix, the operating system, is involved

No wonder most people approach the Net with such dread. Happily, as you will see, the dread is unnecessary.

So, here we go, on to that first step.

CHAPTER 2

WHAT YOU CAN DO WITH INTERNET ACCESS

For most folks, the Internet is a means to an end: communicating with other people or finding information. For others, the Net is an end in itself; legions of users log on and stay there for hours on end.

This semi-aimless Internet wandering and discovering is sometimes referred to as *surfing the Net*. So, what are these people doing, exactly? More specifically, what tools are they using?

Electronic Mail (e-mail): Electronic messages created with e-mail software and sent over the Internet wire and cable system to their destinations, where their recipients can read, print, send, save, or forward those messages to other users.

Mailing Lists: Discussion topic areas which employ the electronic mail system as the means of transmitting an endless stream of opinions and information on about 7,000 different topics.

Newsgroups: Electronic versions of cork bulletin boards to which you post and read messages. Newsgroups store the thoughts and ruminations of millions of users on approximately 12,000 different subjects. You must use a program called a *newsreader,* several of which exist, installed as client software on most Internet providers servers. You can discuss virtually any topic from a to z within the newsgroup system.

Telnet (remote login): The ability to log into a network across the street or on another continent and use it as if you were there on site, from your own computer. Thousands of networks allow "guest" logins, and you can find almost anything from library holdings to Vatican paintings to your local weather forecast.

FTP (file transfer protocol): Almost 1,300 host systems exist as computer file storage sites and allow people to log into those sites and transfer copies of the files held there to the users' own computers. These servers hold over two million files and do not charge for the transfer.

Gopher: An ingenious information retrieval program that is menu-based. When you log into a Gopher session, a menu appears on your screen. As you select menu items, you see succeeding menus, layer after layer, until you locate what you want. You might end up with text, which you can save as a permanent file on your computer or print or forward to someone via Internet e-mail. Or, Gopher might offer you a file which you can download to your PC or, on some Windows or Mac-based systems, view in real-time. Or, you might encounter a telnet session that will log you into a remote network somewhere. Gopher is fast, easy to use, and comprehensive.

World Wide Web: An information retrieval medium that has taken the online world by storm and appears to be doing nothing less than redefining how we may get information in the future. Also at stake is how our children will learn, rewriting our notions of books and libraries along the way.

This is revolutionary, not evolutionary, technology. At the center of the Web is *hypertext linking*. You select highlighted words and pictures on your screen, using a computer mouse. Once selected, you get a new screen full of words, pictures, full-motion video presentations, or stereo sound from which to choose. You can select more items, and continue the linking process until you reach the end of the link. Associated with the Web are Web *browsers* (software programs that enable you to view the Web and mine its wonders) such as Netscape and Mosaic.

Archie: Archie accesses searchable catalogs of the files stored on the 1,300 or so ftp host servers, updating 1/30 of them every day. Archie is flexible, so you can hunt for files based on partial or complete file names. You can access Archie by several means (telnet, Gopher, the World Wide Web, or as client software on your provider's host).

Veronica: Veronica is a search device that examines the menus of all the Gopher servers for keywords. For example, if you issued the keyword *radio* to Veronica, it would report all the Gopher servers that had something to do with radio. You access Veronica as a Gopher menu item.

WAIS: WAIS stands for Wide Area Information Server. WAIS consists of near-ly 500 special document servers that allow you to search for data or keywords within the documents themselves, not just on top level menu or title data. The easiest access to WAIS is through a Gopher menu.

Knowbot/Netfind/Whois: These programs help you find someone's e-mail address. The best way to get that information is to ask the person directly, but white and yellow page data are becoming more complete as time passes.

Internet Relay Chat: IRC makes live keyboard-based "chatting" possible. Once connected, whatever you type and send from your keyboard all other connected people will see.

Keep in mind that this book presents more detail on all of these tools, starting in Part 2. Not only will you learn something more about them, but you will see actual step-by-step instructions and commands to hasten your the road to Net expertise!

CHAPTER 3
HOW DIFFERENT COMPUTERS CAN COMMUNICATE WITH EACH OTHER

The next several chapters feature Internet basics posed in the form of questions and answers that flow logically from one topic to the next.

Q. What kind of computers connect to the Internet?

A. All kinds, from mainframes to notebooks. IBM and IBM-based personal computers. Macs. Sun and Next workstations. DEC mini-computers. Old computers. New computers. And they all communicate and understand one another!

Q. How can this be? I thought, for example, that IBMs and Macs couldn't talk to each other.

A. In 1982, the Internet software wizards created a program called **TCP/IP**, or Transmission Control Protocol/Internet Protocol. TCP/IP breaks Internet-bound messages and files into electronic "packets", puts the packets into electronic envelopes coded with source and destination information, ships those envelopes through the Internet wiring system, and delivers them to your computer, intact and in order.

The beauty of TCP/IP is that it works on almost every computer involved in networking and communication. So, as long as your computer or your Internet access host's computer can run TCP/IP software, you can communicate with every other computer so connected.

Q. So, how does TCP/IP work?

A. Oversimplifying things for the sake of our discussion, the **TCP** part of TCP/IP breaks outbound Internet traffic into packets. It places these packets of data into their own electronic envelopes, then hands the envelopes over to the **IP** part of TCP/IP. The IP part of TCP/IP then "routes" packets to their destination, employing special computers called **routers** along the way over the countless miles of copper wire and fiber-optic cable (the Internet highway).

Routers read the Internet destination address of the envelopes and, if the envelopes' destination address happens to belong to the computer associated with a particular router, the router sends those envelopes on to that computer, where TCP takes the data packets out of their envelopes and puts them back together at the destination computer. Otherwise, the router hands the envelopes off to yet another router until they arrive at the exact destination router.

Now, if an envelope or two runs into a dead end along the router system, let's say a router is disabled or temporarily "down", the IP program quickly reroutes the envelopes to another set of routers until the envelopes reach their destination. See Figure 3-1.

Another important factor about TCP/IP is this: If your computer runs the TCP/IP program, it can have its own, unique Internet address and domain name (which we'll discuss later). It is this software that gives a host the ability to be "on the Internet"; that is, have direct addressing access to the Internet backbone system and all the associated routers.

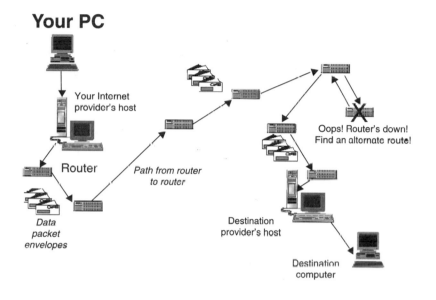

Figure 3-1

CHAPTER 4
ABOUT NETWORKS, CLIENTS, AND SERVERS

Q. What is a computer network?

A. A computer network is a group of connected computers, generally with a central computer called a **server** and connected **client** computers. We may also refer to a server as a *host*. In the client/server relationship, each may share the processing load so that one is not doing a disproportionate amount of work.

The goals of a computer network are:

• Share information. The server may store financial records or other kinds of organized data to which all connected client machines could have access.

• Share hardware. A network might have one expensive, high-speed printer to which all client computers could use.

• Allow client computers to pass messages and data to and from one another.

See Figure 4-1.

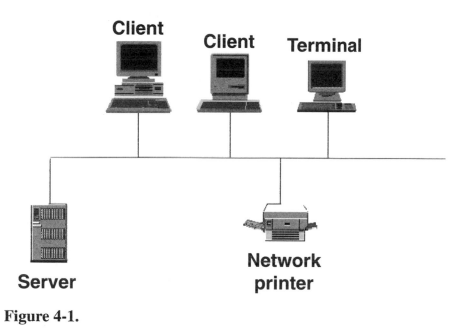

Figure 4-1.

Because you may run into it: A network in which any connected computer can be a client or a server is called a **peer-to-peer** network.

BEYOND THE BORDERS

Consider, for a moment, the network from Figure 4-1. It is totally self-contained and has no provision for access to and from outside that network's confines. All client machines can access common hardware hooked to this network, use the data stored on its server, share some data with other connected client computers, and send electronic mail to all other internal client machines.

Useful, but limited, as you will see.

Now, consider the implications of adding a **gateway** that is connected to the Internet backbone and permits access to and from the outside world — thousands of other networks and millions of individual computers, for example. Suddenly, the client machines on this network can access the information stored on outside networks and individual computers, and can send electronic messages to them. Further, those millions of other systems can access this network's server and use the data on it as well as sending electronic mail to the network's client machines and users. Voila — you have the principle behind the Internet. If the server is running TCP/IP software and has the requisite routers and other associated hardware, it will be so connected. Over 40,000 networks around the world provide gateways to the global Internet system.

See Figure 4-2.

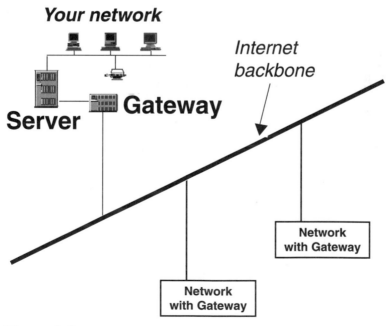

Figure 4-2.

CHAPTER 5

THE INTERNET HIGHWAY WIRING SYSTEM AND TYPES OF ACCESS

Q. What kinds of connections are involved with the Internet?

A. Basically, host servers hook to routers, and routers connect one to another with high and medium speed copper and fiber-optic wires. Think of the wires as highway roadbeds, the routers as highway interchanges, and the host machines hooked to the routers as towns you wish to reach.

The newest "highway road" transmission lines use fiber-optic cable and specialized routers, and can transmit data packets as fast as 2.49 billion bits per second (BPS)! These are few and far between, but will become more prevalent as time goes on. For now, the major high-speed **backbone** highway system consists of **T3** lines that carry data at 45 million BPS. **T1** lines (1.54 million BPS) branch off the T3 lines. **56K** lines (57,600 BPS) branch off the T1s. Finally, there are 28,800 and 14,400 BPS lines.

In addition to the system just described, there is **ISDN** (Integrated Services Digital Network), which has two 64,000 BPS digital lines that can be used individually or combined into a single 128,000 BPS digital line. We emphasize the digital nature of these lines because digital transmission is almost completely free of the line noise and anomalies that can plague the other analog lines defined above.

To bring some real definition to these line speeds, suppose you wanted to transfer a 16 megabyte file to your computer. Here is how long you would wait for the transfer to complete at the different line speeds:

MEDIUM	SPEED	TRANSFER TIME
OC-48	2.49 billion BPS	< 1 second
T3	45 million BPS	2.8 seconds
T1	1.54 million BPS	1.3 minutes
ISDN	64,000 BPS	33.3 minutes
56K	57,600 BPS	38 minutes
28.8K*	28,8000 BPS	1.25 hours
14.4K*	14,400 BPS	2.5 hours

* Generally, through a modem hooked to your computer.

Q. What is bandwidth?

A. **Bandwidth** is *potential*, and is a function of line speed as well as router and modem capability. Consider these methods of transmitting water: a straw, a garden hose, a fire hose, a city water line. There is only so much water you can force through each medium, but each succeeding mode of transmission has much greater potential than its predecessor.

And so it is with the copper and fiber lines that carry Internet traffic. Obviously, having a 56K line feeding your computer is vastly superior to having 14.4K access through a modem. One obstacle, as always, is money. 56K dedicated access is fast, but more expensive than what you'd pay using a modem with 14.4K access.

Q. What kinds of connections and access exist?

A. Several. Let's begin with the most sophisticated and expensive means of access.

1. **A T1 leased line.** With a T1 line, you have outstanding speed and bandwidth which you can distribute to your organization via a local area network. Large and medium size companies, Internet resellers, universities, and other organizations which have large bandwidth requirements or which need to give large groups of people Internet service, buy this access. Hosts that have T1 connections run TCP/IP software and have their own Internet addresses and domain names (both of which we'll discuss in Chapter 7). This access is available from Internet resellers and costs several thousand dollars per month. The phone company must run a special line to your site.

Another consideration here is hardware. If you're going to redistribute this connectivity, you'll need a muscular host server with lots of system memory (RAM) and several gigabytes of hard drive storage. Many T1 sites use an array of networked computers, each of which is assigned a certain task. You will also need a router and a digital converter[1] (a device that allows routers to talk to each other). At your option, you may also install a "firewall" computer that will be your line of defense against outside hackers you don't want spooking around your system. The tab for this hardware armada: tens of thousands of dollars.

As you can see in Figure 5-1, your network, firewall, router, and digital converter system use a T1 line to tie to a major national **Network Service Provider** (NSP). NSPs are the primary links to the backbone system. MCI, Sprint, AT&T, the Regional Bell Operating Companies (Baby Bells), UUNET, BBN, PSI, and ANS are some of the principal NSPs.

---

[1] Technically called a CSU/DSU, for Channel Service Unit/Digital Service Unit.

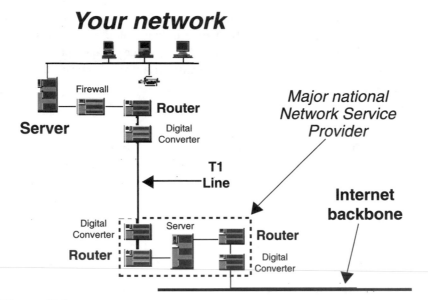

Your network

Firewall

Server   **Router**

Digital Converter

T1 Line

Digital Converter

Server

Router   **Router**

Digital Converter

Major national Network Service Provider

Internet backbone

Figure 5-1

18

2. **A 56K leased line**. At first glance, 56K dedicated leased line service appears to be much the same as T1 service, only slower. To some extent, this is true. A 56K line, hardwired to your site, offers decently fast service, but distribution of the signal around a network may be restricted because you simply do not have the bandwidth of a T1 connection. But, not to worry. If all your site needs is 56K service, you will have acceptable bandwidth. As with the T1 line, you'll need the router, digital converter, and, for some, the firewall, but the per-month line charges for 56K service are far less expensive ($500 to $1,000 per month). Some individuals buy 56K lines and less expensive routers and digital converters (and they sometimes dispense with the firewall computer altogether), making this a tolerable expense. As with T1 access, hosts connected to 56K lines run TCP/IP software, so have their own Internet addresses and are directly "on the Internet".

3. **ISDN access**. This requires a digital line to your site (something akin to the T1 and 56K lines, only digital, but still hardwired). ISDN service has several advantages over 56K service:

- It is faster.

- Installation and monthly charges can be less expensive. It is digital and therefore noise free.

- There is no requirement for a router and digital converter, which implies the potential disadvantage of not having your machine's own Internet address. You do need special ISDN-related hardware for your computer, but this gear is far less expensive than a router and digital converter.

ISDN has been around for years, but the phone companies have never had a compelling reason to offer it to the general public (or even businesses). With the huge demand for Internet services, ISDN now has a reason for new life. Phone companies as well as Internet providers offer ISDN service.

ISDN offers two channels, called "B" lines, each of which carries data at 64,000 BPS. You can combine the two channels into a single 128K line. Given its speed and inherent digital quality, ISDN is a most attractive service choice.

4. **PPP/SLIP access.** PPP (Point-to-Point Protocol) and SLIP (Serial Line Internet Protocol) service allow individual computers to have their own Internet addresses and puts them "on the Internet" (direct access to the backbones), but they do so through common modems and telephone lines, eliminating the need for routers and digital converters. Personal computers that have PPP or SLIP access run TCP/IP software designed for small computers. This service is non-continuous (if you want on, your TCP/IP software dials in to an Internet provider through your modem). It is also relatively slow, operating at either 14.4K or 28.8K BPS. But, for simple, nondemanding operations, this access is sufficient, inexpensive, and extremely popular, and you get your own domain name and Internet address.

Figure 5-2 demonstrates the PPP and SLIP connection. Note that your PC's modem dials into your Internet provider's modem and the provider's modem connects to a **terminal server**, not a host server that holds terminal emulation client application software. The terminal server passes the modem signal to the provider's router.

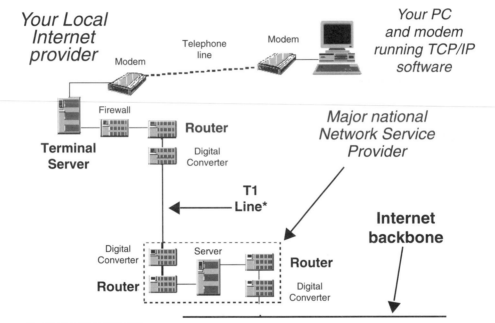

Figure 5-2

5. **Shell account access**. With a shell account, your computer uses a modem, telephone line, and common "terminal emulation" software (Kermit or Procomm Plus, for example) to access a host that has direct Internet access. This level of service does not put your own computer "on the Internet", so it does not have its own, unique Internet address. On the other hand, for most users, this method of access possesses enough features and speed to be more than adequate.

Here's something important to understand: When your modem links your computer to an Internet provider's host, *your computer becomes a terminal attached to that host as if it were hardwired to it*. The prompt that appears on your computer is actually coming from that remote host. So, if you type Pine, Gopher, telnet, ftp, or other commands at your keyboard, you are *issuing commands to and using software installed on that remote host*, but the session is reflected on your screen.

So, when you receive e-mail or get a computer file using file transfer protocol (ftp), the e-mail message file and the computer file end up on that remote host, not on your own computer's hard drive. Again, more on the implications of this later.

Note in Figure 5-3 that the terminal emulation/Unix shell dial-up has a similarity to the PPP/SLIP dial-up. Two differences are that:

• Your PC uses terminal emulation, not TCP/IP, software for modem communications.

• Your Internet provider's modem connects with its host server, not terminal server. The host server holds the client software (the Internet tools) that you require.

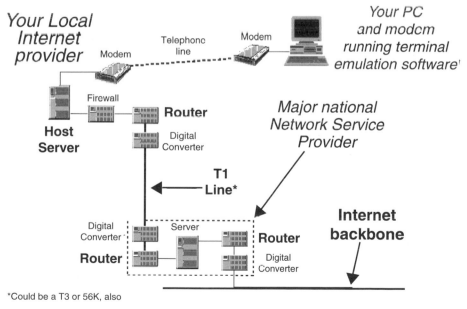

*Could be a T3 or 56K, also

Figure 5-3

21

The term "shell account" comes from what you get when your computer dials into a host system: a Unix prompt associated with a "shell" (another term for "environment").

Put differently, a DOS user boots a PC and gets a C: prompt which comes from the COMMAND.COM file. Unix users boot their systems and get handed to one of several, versatile environments (shells), each with its own features and command structures. Depending on the shell into which you are placed, the prompt you see might be a $, %, or > symbol. So, when you use terminal emulation software to dial into a Unix system, you end up in a shell with a $, %, or > prompt. Your computer is now a temporary terminal on that Unix server, connected via a modem.

We must make this point: there is nothing inferior with using a dial-up shell account. Millions of people, including Internet authors and experts, make this their access of choice. It's fast, inexpensive, and comprehensive.

6. **Terminal access.** Students at universities and employees in corporations may have this rather basic Internet access. These "dumb" terminals are hardwired to physical networks and can only use the client software (Gopher, telnet, e-mail and the others) on the host servers to which they are attached. See Figure 5-4.

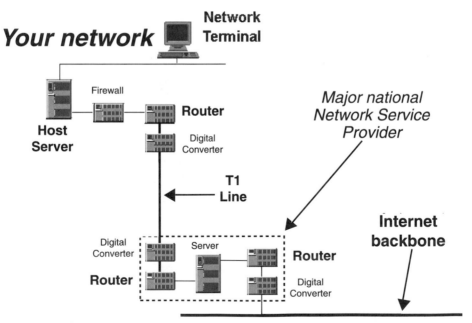

Figure 5-4

7. **BBS access.** Many dial-up electronic bulletin boards offer gateways to Internet services.

To get this kind of access, dial into the BBS. Once connected, look for a menu item that reads "Internet", "Internet Gateway", "Internet Services", or some other, similar entry. Ensure that the BBS is managed and maintained by a sysop who knows a great deal about the Internet and how it works.

If:

- the price is right (and it often is with BBSs),

- the phone number is local (it's your preference to dial long distance to a BBS, but a goal is to minimize expenses),

- there are multiple lines (so you get something other than busy signals),

- and the Internet service is comprehensive, this may be the way to go. Also, you may get 28.8K service. BBS access is worth investigating.

8. **Freenets.** Freenets are locally operated Internet service providers who are sponsored by institutions, often universities. They are easy to use, and some offer a wide range of Internet services. And they cost you nothing out-of-pocket. Freenets can have such drawbacks as a limited number of phone lines (making only a busy signal available to you) or limited Internet service, but the price is right if you're willing to be patient with the service itself and, in most cases, primarily use the freenet for e-mail services.

CHAPTER 6
CHOOSING THE ACCESS THAT'S RIGHT FOR YOU

Q. So, what kind of access should I get?

A. If you are going to use the feed constantly, pass megabits of data in and out during the day, and allow 24-hour access to your site, a 56K leased line or higher is a must. If your Internet connection will be used for non-continuous electronic mail, newsgroup, and World Wide Web activity, a 14.4K dial-up account or ISDN may suffice.

Keep in mind that 56K dedicated leased lines are hard-wired into your site. You cannot take this kind of Internet access on the road with you. So, if you need Internet service while traveling, you should make provisions for modem access from "outside" into your site which will then link you to the Internet.

For most people, access type may be normally defined more by money than by other requirements. Your location might really need a 56K link, but your perceptions or wallet might dictate otherwise and you might settle for a 28.8K dial-up account. In time, though, an upgrade to greater bandwidth might be inevitable.

Q. What is "metering" and why should I be concerned with it?

A. Metering is the practice of charging for Internet access by the minute or hour at a fixed rate for the length of time you are online. Most commercial online companies (America Online, CompuServe, et al) meter for some or all of their services. Since these companies offer Internet access, using them might be an expensive way to use the Internet.

Many Internet service providers (ISPs) do *not* meter. Most charge a reasonable, flat fee, monthly or annually. But the owners of the commercial backbones may impose metering on ISPs who will have no choice but to pass it on to their customers. Nobody knows when metering will begin, but some see its implementation as a given, sooner or later.

Q. How much will I have to pay if the ISPs impose metering?

A. Nobody knows. Conventional wisdom dictates that ISPs don't want to put themselves out of business through excessive pricing, and everyone who believes that metering is inevitable hopes the backbone owners won't charge ridiculous prices for carrying Internet packets.

REFLECTIONS ON ACCESS AND SERVICE

Two of the most important decisions you will make about Internet access will be:

1. Who will provide my service?

2. What kind of service do I need (or want)?

Regarding the first question, that we briefly discussed in the previous chapter and will discuss even more throughout this book, the best advice is to find a provider who: 1. Is local, so you don't have to make a toll or long distance call just to get connected. Failing that, a national provider, such as NetIowa or Uunet/Alternet that offers 800 access (at a price). 2. Offers comprehensive Internet service. 3. Maintains the site, so you don't encounter Internet access that is "down" constantly.

Regarding the second question (what kind of service do I need or want), you have four choices, two of which we will examine in depth throughout this book:

1. A "dumb" terminal, hooked to a network server. You use the software installed in the server, but can do no processing of your own. This is not "home" service, but is associated with university or corporate networks.

2. A freestanding personal computer (IBM or Mac) connected to a server by way of either a network or through a modem through "indirect" terminal emulation. You are in a sort of twilight zone: Your computer can do its own processing, but you are connected to a server and, during that connection, your PC is really nothing more than a terminal hooked to the server, using that server's software (as in our first example, immediately above). The server's software is called client software or a client application. This kind of access is also referred to as terminal emulation access because your computer must pretend to be a terminal hooked to (and at the mercy of) that server.

In this scenario, your PC would use such software as Procomm Plus (for DOS or Windows), Crosstalk, Qmodem, Telix, or some other kind of communication software that offers VT- 100 terminal emulation. It is this kind of access that gives you the Unix shell account. Your PC, even though its operating system is DOS or Mac, is hooked to a server whose operating system is most likely Unix. It could be VMS (which is what Delphi and NetIowa use), but we'll assume Unix for the sake of this tutorial.

But remember: Your PC is a terminal on that server and must use what the server feeds it. If the server uses Unix, it will feed Unix screens (from Unix shells, hence the term "shell account") down the line during your Internet session. Therefore, you will see a Unix prompt (% or $ or >) instead of a DOS C:\> prompt on your screen.

The upside to this type of service is that, given a reasonably fast connection (a 14,400 or 28,800 modem, for example), the service is swift because it is text based (no pictures.. just words on a screen). Also, this service offers a wide variety of tools (E-mail, Gopher, finger, etc.).

The downside is that it is not "direct". Because your PC is acting as a terminal on a server, it is the server that is directly connected to the Internet backbone/router system, not your PC. Therefore, your PC does not have its own Internet address and cannot, for example, download files directly from Internet file servers around the planet to your PC.

This is no cause for despair, however. Unix shell accounts are useful and worthwhile, and millions of folks use them happily every day.

Another important point: If you use graphically based commercial online providers such as America Online, CompuServe, and Prodigy to "gateway" out to Internet services, your PC is still in a terminal emulation environment and will not have its own direct connection or identity, like a Unix shell account. It may be pretty on the monitor screen, but it's still indirect terminal emulation! Again, millions of people access Internet host servers every day using these services, and they don't have any complaints because it's all the service they need. You will see, though, that this might not be the most ideal way to access Internet services.

Further, and this is important, this book assumes that the student is connected to the service via a modem, not a network. Having said that, though, the descriptions of the tools (E-mail, Gopher, and so forth) are still useful and valid whether your access is from a network or a modem. But, we'll assume a modem for the actual type of connection in the terminal emulation arena.

3. A freestanding personal computer (IBM or Mac) connected to a server by way of a modem, but this time with "direct" access to the Internet backbone/router system. Note: Networks can do this, too, but our academic focus here is on modem "dialups".

You have seen that you can use a modem to get to a server that, using that server's client software, allows you to pass data out to and receive data from other computers throughout the Internet system. Recall that this is terminal emulation, and that your PC is not directly connected to other Internet host machines (a host is a computer that offers services or information to other computers).

Now, by simply using a different type of software and by having your Internet provider give you a special connection called a PPP or SLIP account (not a Unix shell account), the same PC and modem you used to dial up to a terminal emulation session and a Unix shell account can instead get "direct" access to the Internet backbone/router system and have its own Internet address and unique Internet identity!

If you need a refresher on PPP and SLIP, step back to the previous chapter. For now, remember that a PPP or SLIP account is more sophisticated and more direct (out to the Internet) than a Unix shell account.

Let's start with your connection software. Instead of using terminal emulation software such as Procomm Plus, use instead special Internet software called TCP/IP software, that, these days, is made for anyone using Microsoft Windows 3.1 or later in 386 Enhanced mode. This is special software that looks for that cryptic PPP or SLIP account, not a Unix shell account. Once it finds either pipeline, your PC is now placed straight through to the Internet router system, and essentially bypasses the host server that held all that client software.

Wait a minute, you say! If I bypass that client software, how will I send e-mail, look at Gopher menus, download files, and so all those other nifty Internet things?

Easy, is the reply. Instead of hunting for client software on some server down the line, all that client application software that makes all the Internet tools work is on your PC ! Note that, for the most part, this application software is Windows based.

So, you use different software to go to a more direct link to the backbones and routers, and application software that makes things like E-mail and Gopher possible. All these are installed on your hard drive. By the way, the Windows-based TCP/IP software on your hard drive has a communication module that dials modems.

Pros and Cons: The upside to a PPP or SLIP connection is that you are in a graphical (Windows or Mac) environment and can use programs such as Netscape and Mosaic to see the Internet in all its full color, stereo sound, motion video glory. You can also have your very own, unique Internet identity (domain name). The author of this tutorial has his own domain name, bgi.com, and receives e-mail at the address pat@bgi. com.

The downside is principally two fold: a. You need a fast computer with lots of system RAM and powerful graphics capability. These machines are not terribly expensive, but still represent an investment that some folks simply cannot afford to make despite the perceived reasonableness of the system price. b. Your PPP or SLIP costs more than a Unix shell account. It's not that much more, but it still is more.

4. Finally, if you are wealthy or hit the lottery, there is the dedicated leased line, a special telephone line that needs expensive peripheral hardware. This tutorial does not go into too much detail on this because people simply cannot afford it and they are interested more in learning about things that they can afford and are of immediate use to them.

CHAPTER 7
INTERNET ADDRESSING

Q. How does Internet addressing work?

A. There are two forms of Internet addressing. The addressing scheme which the Internet routers use is called the **IP** (Internet Protocol) **address**. The IP address consists of four numbers, each in the range of 0 to 255, separated by periods called **dots.** Because of the explosion of Internet interest, Internet engineers are concerned that the current 32-bit system will run out of addresses. Therefore, they are studying an expanded 64-bit addressing scheme that will add more numbers to the string and allow for more addresses.

Each number in the four-digit address is called a **dotted quad**. An example of an IP address is *198.6.245.121*. The Internet routing system maintains tables of information that match IP addresses to their respective host sites; so, if you send data to IP 198.6.245.121, the routing system will find the host that owns that IP address.

Since humans can remember sequences of words and parts of words more easily than numeric strings, the **FQDN** (Fully Qualified Domain Name) system exists to ease the task of locating Internet host sites.

A FQDN is composed of subcomponents, normally in the format *host.site.domain_type*. See Table 7-1.

TABLE 7-1

SUBCOMPONENT	MEANING	EXAMPLE
Host	The name of the host system accepting the Internet traffic sent to the FQDN. Sometimes the host system name is the same as the site name. Sometimes, the host name is omitted from the FQDN.	<any name or word>
Site	The physical location or name of the organization where the host is located.	wright; delphi; wpafb
Domain type	The type of organiztion that operates the host system.	<See Table 7-2>

A subcomponent of the FQDN that gets lots of attention is the **domain type**. There are six principal domain types used in the United States. See Table 7-2.

TABLE 7-2

DOMAIN TYPE	DEFINITION	EXAMPLE
com	A commercial company	netcom.com
edu	An educational institution	osu.edu
gov	A government institution	house.gov
mil	The U.S. military	af.mil
net	An Internet Service Provider	icsi.net
org	Miscellaneous organizations (e.g., Electronic Frontier Foundation or National Public Radio)	eff.org

Table 7-3 offers some simple, but typical, FQDN examples.

TABLE 7-3

bgi.com	A commercial site called *bgi*.
npr.org	The organization *National Public Radio*.
desire.wright.edu	A host computer named "Desire" at Wright State University (Dayton, Ohio), which is an educational institution.

Domain names can vary in length and have several subcomponents. Consider the FQDN *wpgate1.wpafb.af.mil*. That FQDN is a host system called "wpgate1" at Wright-Patterson Air Force Base, an Air Force facility, and definitely associated with the U.S. military.

When domains contain just a site name and a domain type (*delphi.com* or *bgi.com*), one of two conditions is likely to be true: The site is either very large or very small. Large sites, such as Delphi Corporation, route all traffic throughout their systems after the traffic has entered the general domain delphi.com. So, a single-name domain can mask an extensive internal collection of hosts and networks.

Very small sites, such as *bgi.com*, typically have a single computer. With tiny sites such as these, the host name is normally the same as the site name and is usually implied but unwritten. For example, the full name of *bgi.com* is *bgi.bgi.com*. Since the redundancy appears silly, and since there is but a single host system at that site, the FQDN redundancy is eliminated and the host system name is not displayed.

You could address e-mail to *pat@bgi.bgi.com*, but using the shortened version (pat@bgi.com) is preferable and works.

Every FQDN has a corresponding IP address, so you could use either addressing scheme when trying to reach a site (*bgi.com* is *198.6.245.121* and vice-verse). However, a site host could change the IP address associated with a particular FQDN address; the routing tables then would correct the FQDN address to match the new IP address. But, if a person were in the habit of only using IP addressing instead of FQDN addressing, he would find himself suddenly unable to contact the site even though it still existed under its current FQDN name because of the IP name change.

The domain type format you just learned is for U.S. addressing. There are dozens of countries outside the U.S. that offer Internet services. The addressing format for non-U.S. countries:

- might not use the three-letter domain type (e.g., edu, com, etc.) and
- substitutes a two-letter format. The two letters correspond to the country (i.e., *ca* for Canada, *uk* for Great Britain, *au* for Australia, and so forth). This addressing takes this form:

<host>.site.country.

The non-U.S. country code is always two letters. Finally, on rare occasions, you might see *.us* in a United States-based address.

CHAPTER 8
THE HARDWARE YOU NEED

Q. I have an old PC I bought in 1985. I still use it for lots of simple applications I know and love. Can I use this PC to use Internet services?

A. Technically, yes, but you won't want to do this for long. Until mid-1993, Internet traffic was all text-based, just words on a screen. In 1993, a program called Mosaic, which we will visit later, upped the ante on connectivity. So, retire the old guy and buy a new computer. Don't upgrade, buy a whole new system.

Q. So, what kind of hardware *do* I need?

A. The most important hardware considerations are those that affect how quickly data bits move into, through, and out of your system. If you do not understand the outline listed here, take it to your favorite computer vendor and show it to him or her. Assuming you use a personal computer for your access, as millions of people do, your system should have:

- A 32-bit "local bus" video card (the component that draws images to your monitor screen) and a *noninterlaced* monitor.

- In an IBM-based PC, a PCI or Vesa Local Bus motherboard.

- In an IBM-based PC, a 16550-series UART chip in your serial port if you use an external modem.

- A SCSI-based or cached IDE disk-drive system with a hard drive with fast data seek and transfer rates.

- A 28.8K modem based on the V.34 specification, if you plan to use dial-up PPP/SLIP or shell access. Skip the 14.4K modems. They are old news now.

- A 16-bit stereo sound card.

- A mouse.

- At least a 256 byte hardware RAM cache.

- At least 8 megabytes (MB) of system RAM, but try to go for 16MB. You'll be glad you did.

Notice that there has been no mention of PowerPC, Pentium, RISC, or 486 CPU chips. Your PC should have the fastest CPU chip you can afford, but realize that a properly configured 486DX2-66 could outperform many Pentium systems sold in discount chain stores.

CHAPTER 9
THE SOFTWARE YOU NEED

Q. What software do I need?

A. Given a personal computer, not a network terminal or minicomputer system, and a connection to a dial-up shell account, any software that offers these three features will suffice:

- *VT-100 terminal emulation.* As we've seen, a dial-up shell account makes your computer a terminal on a provider's host system. More specifically, your computer is pretending to be a *VT-100* terminal, or some close variation thereof, because that's the kind of terminal the host thinks it sees at your end of the line. VT-100 emulation gives you control over screen cursor movement.

- *Zmodem transfer protocol.* For shell dial-ups, transferring files from an Internet host to you is a two-step process, something we'll see in detail later. Zmodem protocol is the tool that transfers a file from your provider's host server to your computer, over the phone line. Another transfer protocol popular in some university systems is Kermit (yes, named after *the* frog). Kermit, however, transfers files much more slowly than Zmodem.

- *A software driver for your specific modem.* Your modem needs the right software commands if it expects your computer to "talk" to another modem and computer across phone lines. Your communication software should include the software code, called a *driver*, for your specific modem. Note: If your Internet access is through a network at school or work, or through a dedicated leased line, you don't have to worry about this.

If your access is via a PPP or SLIP connection, there are several, Windows-based alternatives, among them:

- Spry's *Internet-In-a-Box*

- NetManage's *Internet Chameleon*

- Peter Tattam's shareware, *Trumpet Winsock*

- Netcom's *NetCruiser* if your access is through Netcom, a national Internet provider with access points in most major cities.

Regarding the list of software packages mentioned in the preceding paragraph:

The Spry and NetManage packages are self-contained "suites" that include TCP/IP software and individual client programs that install on your personal computer's hard drive. Remember: With these packages, your PC will run TCP/IP software from its own hard drive, it will have its own Internet address and have direct access to the Internet backbone system. Therefore, the client software to use such services as e-mail, Gopher, telnet, and so on *must reside on your hard drive*, not on a host elsewhere. Put another way: With these software suites, you are not dialing into an Internet provider's system as a terminal, *you are your own Internet location* and *so must have your own client software* to do e-mail, ftp, and so forth. These suites provide all of this. Another thing: These, and the Trumpet Winsock program described next, all use either a PPP or SLIP connection, which is more expensive than a standard, Unix shell account.

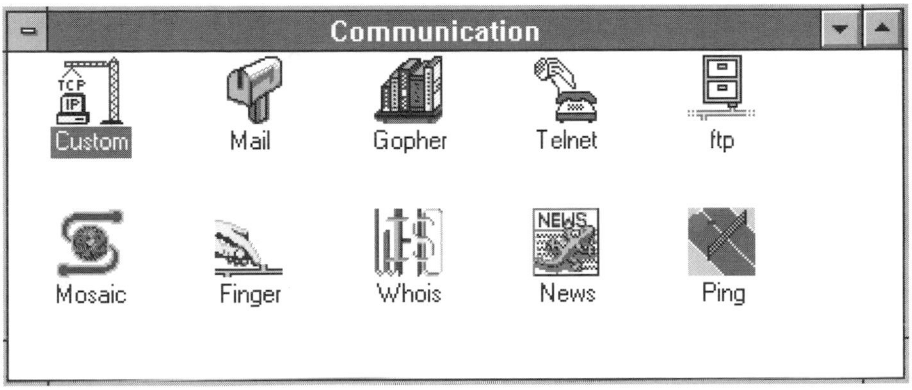

Figure 9-1

Figure 9-1 shows the NetManage Chameleon program group icons. Each icon represents a client program. Note the icons for mail, Gopher, telnet, and ftp. Note also that Mosaic is *not* part of the Chameleon suite although NetManage now has its own Web browser. Windows permits you to add icons to any program group.

Here's how those client programs work in TCP/IP-based Windows packages. In Figure 9-2, client software for such activities as e-mail, telnet, and ftp is stored on the PC's hard drive. You can load e-mail client software from your hard drive, create a message, then send it to a recipient somewhere else on another system that has Internet access.

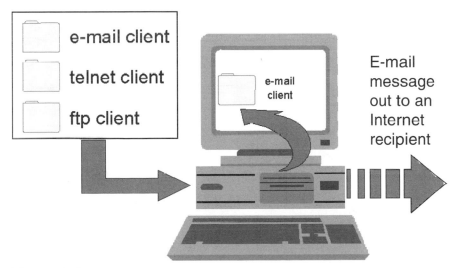

Figure 9-2

Note: *Trumpet Winsock* is just TCP/IP software and includes no application client software. It needs additional client programs to use e-mail, Gopher, etc., and those are available as *shareware* or *freeware* programs from various Internet sites. Obviously, this is not terribly convenient, as you have to piece together lots of different programs. But, the price for all this might be far less than the Spry and NetManage packages. So, the decision is between convenience and money.

WINDOWS SOCKETS (WINSOCK)

Trumpet Winsock comes with a file called **WINSOCK.DLL**, that is very crucial to TCP/IP access from PCs running Microsoft Windows. The Spry, NetManage, and Trumpet programs all need (and include) their own versions of WINSOCK.DLL as a sort of "middle-man" that allows the Windows-based client programs for e-mail, Gopher, and so forth to communicate with the TCP/IP program running your Internet link.

In Figure 9-3, the Windows-based client software installed on your hard drive uses WINSOCK.DLL to call upon the Windows-based TCP/IP software (also on your hard drive) to process[2] whatever the client software needs (send an e-mail message, find an ftp host system, whatever). Of course, this is exactly what TCP/IP software on host servers does, too, only you're doing it locally, on your PC.

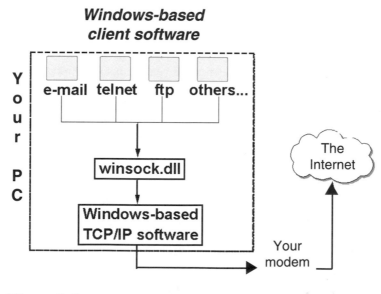

Figure 9-3

---

[2]Break into packets, place into electronic "envelopes", and send to the Internet backbone.

OTHER INTERFACES AND GATEWAYS TO
INTERNET HOSTS AND SERVICES

Netcruiser, the "front end" for the Internet provider Netcom, is a Windows-based program that presents all Internet tools on one convenient screen instead of utilizing a collection of individual icons. Figure 9-4 demonstrates the compact nature of the Netcruiser interface. Note the row of icons above the map of the United States. These icons launch such applications as e-mail, the World Wide Web, and Gopher.

The file transfer protocol, telnet and Gopher applications present a map of the United States. When you click your mouse on one of the states, the ftp and telnet resources appear in a list. When you click on a name from the list, Netcruiser takes you to that host.

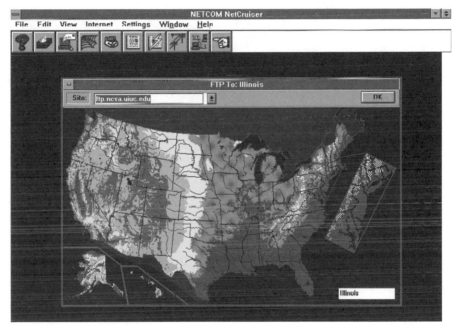

Figure 9-4

Some Internet gateways, America Online and Prodigy, for example, require their own communication software. Others, such as CompuServe, don't necessarily need it, but it is highly recommended. Figure 9-5 shows the Internet gateway screen in America Online.

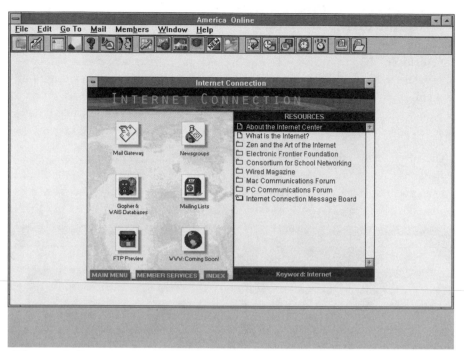

Figure 9-5

CHAPTER 10

WHERE INTERNET SERVICE COMES FROM

Q. Where does Internet service come from?

A. Remember that, at its core, the Internet is a maze of wires and routers, and that messages and information (why you are even bothering to connect) come from other hosts connected, somehow, to the system. So, we can answer this question with two answers:

- Your immediate Internet data comes from a provider set up especially to receive data from other hosts and feed it to your computer. Your provider has, on one side, a router and digital converter connected to the global backbone system and, on the other side, a modem that links his server with your modem and PC.

- Internet messages and information emanate from other hosts, travel the Internet highway system, and find their way through your provider's system to your computer.

Q. What is the relationship among Internet service providers, America Online, Prodigy, a network at school, and other places that provide Net access?

A. Basically, they all offer you access to other people and resources around the world. The "Big Five" (America Online, CompuServe, Delphi, Genie, and Prodigy) originally existed as self-contained islands of information, entertainment, education, and communication (from member to member). Whatever you needed, weather, sports scores, news, message-passing, and so on, was available from within each service. Most of these commercial services did an admirable job, but their ability to make contact outside of their systems was limited to nonexistent.

In 1992, Delphi opened its doors to the global Internet, offering all Internet communication, searching, and information services to its paying customers through an Internet gateway. Its members could get out to the Internet through the gateway, but non-members out in Internet-land could not get in[3]. By 1995, the floodgates opened, and most of the Big Five finally offered comprehensive outbound Internet access.

With this background, consider the following entities:

- A dial-up customer of a commercial Internet provider whose only business is connecting customers out to the Net system,

- A customer of any of the Big Five commercial online companies just discussed,

---

[3] A fine point of detail: People with Delphi accounts who also have Internet access from other sources can use telnet to enter the Delphi gateway from another Internet point. CompuServe offers this access to its paying members, also.

- A member of a free-standing bulletin board service,

- A student with terminal access at a university,

- An employee at a company that offers Internet access through a networked company server,

- An administrative assistant of a member of the U. S. House of Representatives.

Each one of those people uses his or her own computer or terminal to access a host machine running TCP/IP. Each TCP/IP host has a router and digital converter that has fiber cable or copper wire access to other routers that eventually lead to the T3 backbone system. So, someone with a Prodigy account can send e-mail to a friend at America Online.

Another factor that makes e-mailing possible from one service using a propri-etary e-mail format to another with its own proprietary format is that gateways *trans-late* the unique standards, or **protocols**, specific to one system into a common Internet e-mail protocol called *Simple Mail Transfer Protocol* (SMTP). Networks and servers that pass Internet e-mail into and out of their proprietary systems "understand" SMTP and translate it into their respective formats. See Figure 10-1.

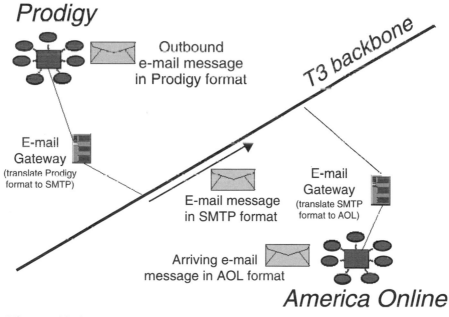

Figure 10-1

CHAPTER 11

OPERATING SYSTEMS AND THE INTERNET

Q. What is an operating system?

A. An operating system is software that acts as an intermediary between your hardware and your application software. Take DOS-based computers, for example. There are thousands of different hardware configurations that all claim to be "IBM-compatible", or the functional equivalent of the IBM-label PC.

Yet, each is asked to run any given application program (a Microsoft Windows word processor, for example) in a predictable fashion. Imagine the how chaotic the application software business would be if Microsoft had to create a version of Word for Windows for all the different hardware configurations that exist! The operating system, however, smooths the way, ensuring that application programs can run on a computer that *is* IBM compatible.

Your computer's operating system "loads" when you turn on your PC. It reads your hardware configuration and gives you a screen prompt and cursor. When you load application software, it helps your hardware execute instructions because it balances what hardware exists to what the application program expects to see.

Q. How many operating systems exist now?

A. More than you think. Some major ones are MS DOS, PC DOS, Novell DOS, OS/2, Windows NT, and so many versions of Unix that keeping track is difficult. Microsoft Windows and Windows for Workgroups are not operating systems. They are graphical shells for DOS, but have special memory and hardware management talents that exceed the capabilities of DOS.

Q. Why is Unix associated with the Internet?

A. Unix is a *multi-user* operating system. That is, you can load it to a server, and many users can log into that server and do different things simultaneously[4]. This ability has obvious benefits in a multi-user situation. Consider the implications of each user dialing up to his or her own server at a provider's site!

Also, Unix was the operating system in use on some of the machines on which "internetting" was invented.

Q. I've heard that there are several variations of Unix. Do they all do the same thing?

A. For the sake of your Internet shell account, and assuming that you do not intend to learn and use all the features that exist for all the shells and brands of Unix, you can feel comfortable that the commands listed in Table 11-1 will work in a predictable fashion regardless of the brand of Unix or shell you might encounter.

---

[4]DOS is a *single-user* operating system and, in many ways, is clearly inferior to Unix. Unix predates DOS by several years but never caught on in the consumer market; exactly *why* this happened is the subject of legend and books.

For the curious, here are some different Unix flavors:

UNIX NAME	ASSOCIATED COMPANY
AIX	IBM Corp.
BSD	Berkeley Software Design
Linux	Publicly developed
Nextstep	NeXT
Solaris	Sun Microsystems
SunOS	Sun Microsystems
System V	AT&T
Ultrix	DEC

(Source: *A Student's Guide to Unix*, H. Hahn, 1993, McGraw-Hill)

Q. What Unix commands do I need to know?

A. Very few. One of the myths of the Internet is that you have to be a Unix expert to use Internet services.

Table 11-1 lists commands that are handy to know.

DOS UNIX COMMAND CROSS-REFERENCE

DOS	UNIX
Change directory: cd\	**cd /** note: Forward slash and space between cd and /
Change directory: cd..	**cd ..** note: space between cd and ..
copy the contents of a file to another file name: copy <file a><file b>	**cp** <file a><File b>
Delete a file: del <file>	**rm** <file>
List all the contents of a directory: dir *.*	**ls** -al
List the contents of a directory and control screen scrolling: dir /p	**ls** *al* |more note: -al is optional here
Move a file from one path to another: move <drive:\path\file><drive:\path>	**mv** <file> <new_path>
Rename a file: rename <old_name><new_name>	**mv** <old_name> <new_name>
List the contents of a file: type <file>	**cat** <file>
List the contents of a file and control screen scrolling: type <file> |more	**cat** <file> |**more** **more** <file>

Table 11-1

Q. Unix is "case-sensitive". What does that mean?

A. It means that you should type upper and lower case letters in Unix file names exactly as you see them. A file name of *My_Data.txt* has a mix of upper and lower case letters, and if you type *my_data.txt* for the file name, the Unix system will not respond to it. The same holds true for subdirectory names on Unix hosts. If you see a capital letter, type a capital letter. DOS is an operating system that is *not* case-sensitive, so most new Internet users who come from a DOS background have some problems with file and directory names.

Q. Unix uses "long" file names. What does that mean?

A. DOS has a strict (limited) file naming convention. The file name cannot have more then eight or fewer than one characters. The file name extension (that part of the file name after the .) can have zero to three characters. That's it.

Unix, on the other hand, uses file names that DOS cannot understand but that are much more descriptive. *My-Data_Jan-Feb.1995.txt* is a legal Unix file name and is more helpful than *1995data.txt*.

Q. I have a DOS PC. What happens when I dial into a shell account?

A. Your DOS computer becomes a terminal on (probably) a Unix system[5]. To get around in your Unix shell, you'll need to use Unix commands. Two excellent books that introduce Unix to unfamiliar users are Harley Hahn's "A Student's Guide to Unix" and "The Waite Group 's Unix Primer Plus".

Q. How do I use Windows to access the Internet?

A. There are two ways to do this. First, you can use Windows-based terminal emulation software such as Procomm Plus for Windows. This will give you access to a Unix shell account. Second, you can use Windows-based TCP/IP software that puts you directly on the Internet backbone.

As with DOS-based terminal emulation software, Windows-based terminal emulation software will allow your PC to be a VT-100 terminal and will use the application software installed on the server to which it dialed. What you type at your keyboard and what you see on your monitor actually happens on the provider's server.

Windows based terminal emulation software offers several advantages, among them:

---

[5]Sometimes you connect to a VMS system. These commands are more DOS-familiar.

- Cut and paste: One of the fundamental advantages of Windows-based applications is the ability to highlight text, copy it to a temporary (and invisible to you) buffer called a *clipboard*, and paste it to another document, either in the same application program or a different one. This is handy for moving text between e-mail messages and word processing documents, for example.

- Scroll back buffer: Sometimes, you need to see information that has scrolled off the screen. Most Windows-based terminal emulation packages offer a "scroll back buffer" that allows you to climb back up through several lines of text that have rolled off the top of the screen.

With the TCP/IP software, your PC uses application software associated with your TCP/IP program and installed on *your* hard drive. You could access either a PPP or SLIP connection. TCP/IP software suites such as NetManage Chameleon allow you to open several applications at once, since those applications are on your hard drive and Windows can open more than one application simultaneously.

Q. What will the impact of Windows95 be to Internet connectivity?

A. Enormous. Windows95 is an operating system that has TCP/IP software embedded into the operating system code. All you'll need to do is add your own shareware applications for e-mail, the World Wide Web, and so on, and you'll be in business. Also, Microsoft hard-coded connectivity to the *Microsoft Network*, its own online service, into Windows95. Add its user-friendly interface, and Windows95 will be an impressive player in the software game.

CHAPTER 12
CONTROLLING THE INTERNET

Q. Who owns the Internet?

A. Nobody. There is no Internet, Inc., no President of the Internet, and no nation on this planet that totally controls all Internet activity.

The closest entity to overall management is **The Internet Society**, a non-profit group that maintains and encourages technical and behavioral standards that affect the Internet as a whole. **The Internet Architecture Board** and **The Internet Engineering Task Force** are two key elements in the continuing effort to coordinate international developments in the technology that allows Internet tools to function seamlessly. Anyone can belong to the Internet Society by paying annual dues.

The Internet is a paradox: controlled anarchy. If elements of the legislature of one country try to make laws to influence the Internet activities of its citizens, the citizens can use foreign resources to accomplish whatever online goals they have, beyond the reach of their government.

Q. How is behavior on the global Internet controlled?

A. Remember, the Internet's resources are scattered over four million hosts and tens of thousands of networks. Each host owner establishes its own guidelines for using its resources; violate the guidelines, and you don't get to use the resources anymore. Your Internet provider is responsible for enforcing the proper behavior of the users to whom it grants access, and uses those guidelines as a yardstick against which to measure proper and improper Internet use.

Because you're probably wondering: The guidelines are surprisingly consistent. Here are two acts that will get you into trouble with your Internet provider, the host systems you would affect, and the Internet users who see such activity:

- Broadcasting unsolicited commercial cold-call ads or religious/political messages indiscriminately to every newsgroup and mailing list you can hit. This very thing got two Arizona immigration attorneys into unprecedented deep yogurt with virtually every aspect of the Internet. It's tempting, but don't ever do it.

- Posting a message inappropriate to the topic of a newsgroup and mailing list. Don't post your ad for lifetime light bulbs in a bee-keeping newsgroup.

You should now have a firm grasp on Internet basics. It's time to learn how to use the major Internet tools. You should have live Internet access in order to get the most from the rest of this book. Just follow the keystrokes in the instructions, and you should be productive very quickly. As you desire and require, spread your wings and try more sophisticated actions. Remember: You can usually type HELP or refer to keystroke combinations that may display on your screen. With that in mind, let's move on!

PART 2
The Internet Through Terminal Emulation

CHAPTER 13
LOGGING IN

You learned in Part 1 that Unix is a multi-user operating system. Since more than one person may be active on the same host server at the same time, each user must log in with his or her own unique login identification, or **login ID**. Upon entering your Internet provider's system, you will see a prompt asking for this ID.

Your login ID is one that the institution assigned or one that you hand-picked. The login ID will be unique and will likely form part of your Internet electronic mail address. So, a careful choice of ID, if a choice exists, is important because that login ID will be another user's first impression of you! If you want to be taken seriously, an ID of `jsmith` is more impressive than `toxic_avenger` (although not as much fun).

After entering a login ID, you will then see a prompt asking for a **password**. Always keep your password a secret, and never give it to anyone. The best passwords are easy to remember, do not need to be written down, and are not easily discovered. Never pick a password based on an object or person closely identified with you.

After entering a password, you learned that you will encounter a Unix prompt. Sometimes the host system will present a friendly menu, but you should be ready to deal with just a %, $, or > prompt.

Some people freeze at the sign of the prompt. One reason for this reaction, aside from Unix being new to most computer users, is a lack of planning; they did not have a course of action ready once they were to start a session. While few people need to choreograph their every move, each person should have a general idea of the goal of each session and what keystrokes he or she might have to use. A little planning and some keystroke research, if new to a system, go a long way toward neutralizing any apprehension about a session. To get help from the Unix operating system, type `help` or `man`, for manual , then hit `<Enter>`.

Something to try: If you want to see who is logged onto your system with you, type `who` and hit `<Enter>`. Then, if you want to chat with one of them live via the keyboard and screen, type   `talk <their_user_ID>`, and hit `<Enter>`. Once the other party enters your talk session, anything that both of you type will appear on the screen! To exit the talk session, hit the `Ctrl-C` keystroke combination (also referred to as `^C`).

The instructions in Part 2 are valid no matter what kind of environment you're using. DOS, Windows, OS/2, and the Mac all work because this is terminal emulation—your computer is a terminal on a host server. And don't forget to set your emulation to VT-100!

An important point: Part 2 describes how to use Internet tools by way of terminal emulation. It does not describe the exact steps to get to Internet services by way of dedicated lines, dumb terminals, or bulletin board systems. However, once you have arrived into such services as Gopher, ftp, and telnet, the keystroke commands specific to those tools are the same no matter how you got there. So, once you're into a service such as Gopher, hitting q to quit is the same if you got there from terminal emulation, a dedicated line, or a BBS.

CHAPTER 14
ELECTRONIC MAIL

E-mail is the most common starting point for all Internet newcomers and perhaps the most important Internet tool because communication is the cornerstone of the Internet. Nearly a dozen mail reader programs exist, but this part focuses on two—a standard Unix mail program called **mailx** and **Pine**.

E-MAIL TIPS

Here are some tips to keep in mind when using the e-mail system:

- Put something meaningful in the *Subject:* line. Useful Subject line contents help call attention to your message. Note: Some people merely scan their incoming mail Subject titles, but might not read all the mail they receive.

- Remember that your e-mail could be forwarded or printed for posterity. Never send anything in the heat of emotion that could come back to haunt you later. Also, never send a message you don't wish repeated.

- The only mandatory e-mail header data is the *To*: field.

- When you sign up with a provider, read its e-mail FAQs (Frequently Asked Questions). Learn the basic rules of the road before sending e-mail.

- Make your e-mail worthwhile. Messages with text bodies that just say "I agree" are a waste of time and resources. This is especially nettlesome on mailing lists and newsgroups which carry substantial traffic.

- Delete old mail. Some providers have a limit on how many bytes they will store or process before they impose storage charges.

FLAME WARS

Flames are vicious, insulting messages. **Flame wars** are flames that people hurl back and forth at each other. It is best to avoid flame wars. If you see something personal or political that irritates you, the best course of action is to not react at that moment. Get away from your computer, talk with a friend, or otherwise vent your passion in a direction that will neither create nor escalate a situation. Remember: You won't change your opponent's mind, your blood pressure will increase, and the whole situation could degenerate into lawsuits.

SIGNATURE FILES

Signature files, or **sigs**, are personalized, sometimes lengthy, descriptions that accompany a person's name at the end of an e-mail or newsgroup message. An example of a sig is:

```
Patrick J. Suarez
Author:  The Beginner's Guide to the Internet
Tutorial software for DOS, Windows, and Mac
E-mail: pat@bgi.com
```

Sigs can contain the person's e-mail address, postal address, phone number, fax number, a quote or witticism, and even a collection of ASCII symbols that create a rough drawing (e.g., a cat, a person riding a bike, the skyline of Milwaukee). The rule of thumb states that sigs over six lines are aggravating.

CREATING NEW MAIL

1. To begin a Unix mail session, you log into a Unix host. If your access is through a dial-up provider, begin a dial-up session.

2. When prompted, enter your `login ID`, then hit `<Enter>`.

3. When prompted for a `password`, type it and hit `<Enter>`.

4. A Unix prompt (**$, %, >**) will appear.

5. Type `mail <addressee>`, where *<addressee>* is the e-mail address of the person with whom you wish to correspond (i.e., *johndoe@host.place.edu*), then hit `<Enter>`.

6. A **Subject**: prompt will appear. Type something appropriate, then hit `<Enter>`.

7. Now you are ready to type your message. Type your text.

8. When you finish typing your message, hit `<Enter>` to go to a new, blank line.

9. If you are unhappy with your message, erase it by typing the `^c` key combination <u>twice</u>. (^ = the Control key) Your message will disappear.

10. If you are happy with your message, type `^d`. The message will send and you will see **EOT** after your last typed line. See Figure 14-1.

```
> Mail ron@erinet.com
Subject: Software OK?

Ron,

Hope all is going well there.

As soon as we get the go-ahead from you, we'll start producing the
copies of BGI/Win for your customers.  Luke has the review disks.

Talk soon!

Pat
EOT
>
```

Figure 14-1

GETTING NEW MAIL

1. Log into the system (see steps 1—4 above).

2. If someone has sent you a message, or other mail has arrived for you, you will see the message **You have new mail**.

3. If you see this, type `mail` and hit `<Enter>`. Your prompt will change to a **&**.

4. A list of new mail will appear. The list will be numbered (look at the left margin of the screen). Hitting `<Enter>` will bring up the text of the first message. Or, you may simply type the number listed at the left margin, and the text of that message will appear. See Figure 14-2. Note: Your message will include a **header** that shows who sent the message, when they sent it, and about a dozen lines of routing information, most of which will be of no interest to you. The text you *are* interested in is below all that header data.

5. After you read a message, type R at the prompt and hit `<Enter>`. (Note the upper case R; Unix is case-sensitive, meaning that if Unix is looking for a capital letter and you type lower case, or vice-versa, you may get an error or nothing will happen.) The R signals Unix mail to begin a reply to the addressee only. If your message and reply had more than one addressee, r would reply to all of them. Note: On some Unix mail programs, R and r have reverse meanings!

6. The screen will change, with the To: address already filled in and the Subject: line also filled in. You are then ready to type a reply. Check the validity of the To: address; sometimes the address is incomplete and must be corrected manually.

7. Try this: With your cursor in column one on the screen, type ~m (~ is the key next to the **1** key). ~m brings the message to which you are replying into the message on which you are currently working! Now, type ~c. That will bring in the Unix editor, and you will be able to move the cursor up and down throughout the original text you imported into your current message. This will allow you to intersperse comments throughout the text you imported. Each line of the original message text has a > symbol in column one. See Figure 14-3.

8. Finish your reply, go to a blank line, then type either ^c twice to cancel the reply or ^d to send it.

9. When you have finished reading all your messages, the keystrokes d*n*, where *n* is the number of the message, will delete the messages from the system.

10. Log out of mail by entering `quit` at the **&** prompt. Your prompt will change back to the standard Unix system prompt.

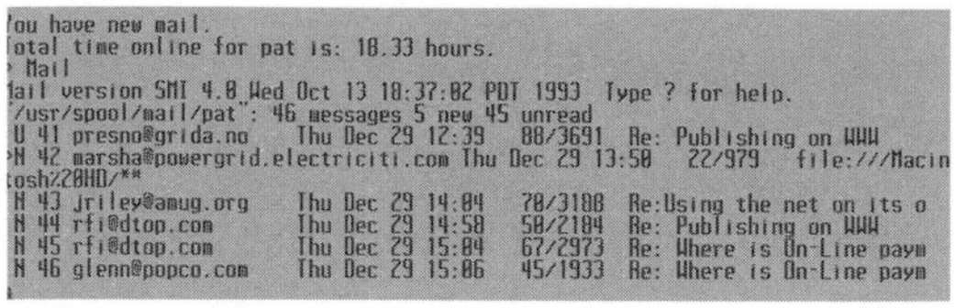

Figure 14-2

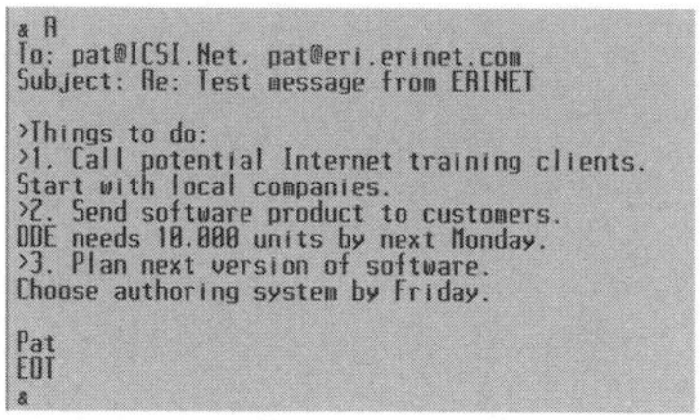

Figure 14-3

PINE MAIL

For beginners, using mailx can be a pain until it has been mastered. There are lots of commands that the user must issue in a careful sequence, and nothing is very intuitive. That's why the mail reader Pine was created.

Developed at the University of Washington, Pine is an e-mail program that gives Unix mail a user-friendly interface. Instead of using the alphabet soup of Unix mail reading and writing commands, you follow simple menu commands in a friendly interface to process Internet mail. The control character (^) is the prefix for some of the commands; other Pine commands use stand-alone letters without the prefix. This powerful, full-featured e-mail program is available on most host systems that offer Internet access, so you probably won't have to grope your way through mailx. Taking a little time to learn Pine's friendly command structure, most of which is available at the bottom of each Pine screen, will yield benefits in time saved reading, creating, replying to, storing, and printing your e-mail!

CREATING E-MAIL WITH PINE

1. At the system prompt, type `Pine` and hit `<Enter>`.

2. If you plan to create mail, select **C** from the main Pine menu[6] See Figure 14-4.

3. After a few seconds, the create menu appears. Fill in the **To:**, **Cc:**, **Attachment:**, and **Subject:** fields, as required. (At a minimum, you will enter something in **To:** and **Subject:**. **Cc:** allows you to send your message to an additional user. **Attachment:** allows you to attach a text file to your message.) Move from field to field with the down and up arrow keys.

---

[6]Three important menu items are **C** to compose new messages; **L** to select which folder you wish to view (folders hold messages you've read and saved as well as messages you've created; you can create your own custom folders, too); and **I** to view incoming messages. **Q** exits Pine.

4. Arrow down to the text body field. Type your text. Pine features "word-wrap" which automatically moves the cursor to succeeding lines without having to hit the <Enter> key. Pine also allows you to move throughout the text you are typing if you wish to edit what you have written. See Figure 14-5.

5. If you do not want to send the message you have created, hit ^c and answer "yes" to the verification prompt.

6. If you want to send your message, hit ^x and answer "yes" to the verification prompt. Pine sends copies of sent mail to the *Sent-Mail* folder so that you can review at a later time messages you have sent. You can also print your outgoing message by selecting that message stored in Sent- Mail, then hitting Y (Print). Remember: You select folders using the **L** selection at the Pine main menu.

7. Hit M to return to the main Pine menu.

8. Hit Q to quit Pine.

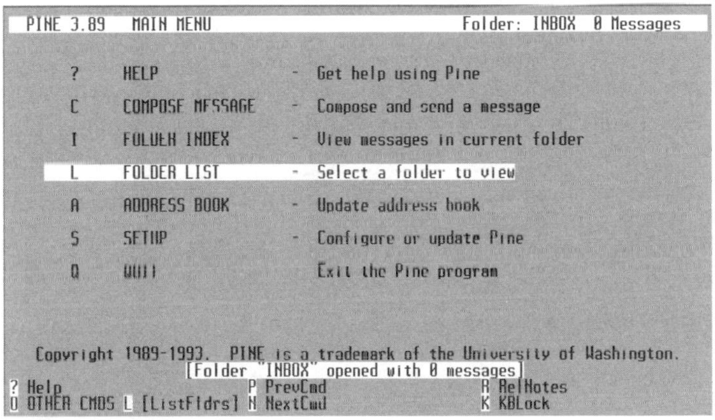

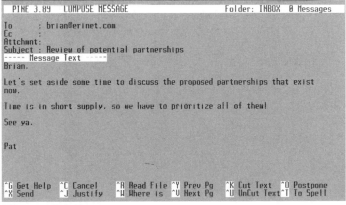

Figure 14-4

Figure 14-5

READING PINE MAIL

1. Enter Pine.

2. If you have new mail waiting, select I to **view** messages in the Inbox folder. Pine identifies each message, one message per line, with its own number. You can either select a number corresponding to the message you wish to read, or hit <Enter> to begin reading all of them. Be sure to refer to the command menu at the bottom of the Pine screen for help with Pine's features. Be sure to delete all read messages by selecting them from the list of messages and hitting D (Delete). See Figure 14-6.

Here is what each symbol in column one means:

• + means that the mail was addressed directly to you

• **N** means you have not yet read the message

• **A** means that you read and answered (replied to) the message

• A blank character means that you read the message but did not reply to it.

3. You can **reply** to a message by hitting R (Reply). Pine will ask if you would like the text body of the message to which you are replying pulled into the reply that you are creating. If you answer "yes", you will be able to intersperse your reply comments throughout the previous message. When you have finished creating your reply, hit ^C to cancel the reply or ^X to send it.

4. You can **print** a message by either selecting it from the list of messages or by entering the message itself, then by hitting Y (Print).

5. You can **save** messages to special folders which you create. To create your own folder, select **L** (Folder List) from the main menu, then **A** (Add a folder). Type the name of the folder, then hit <Enter>. You can then direct messages you have read to archive to that specific folder.

6. Hit M to return to the main Pine menu.

7. Hit Q to quit Pine.

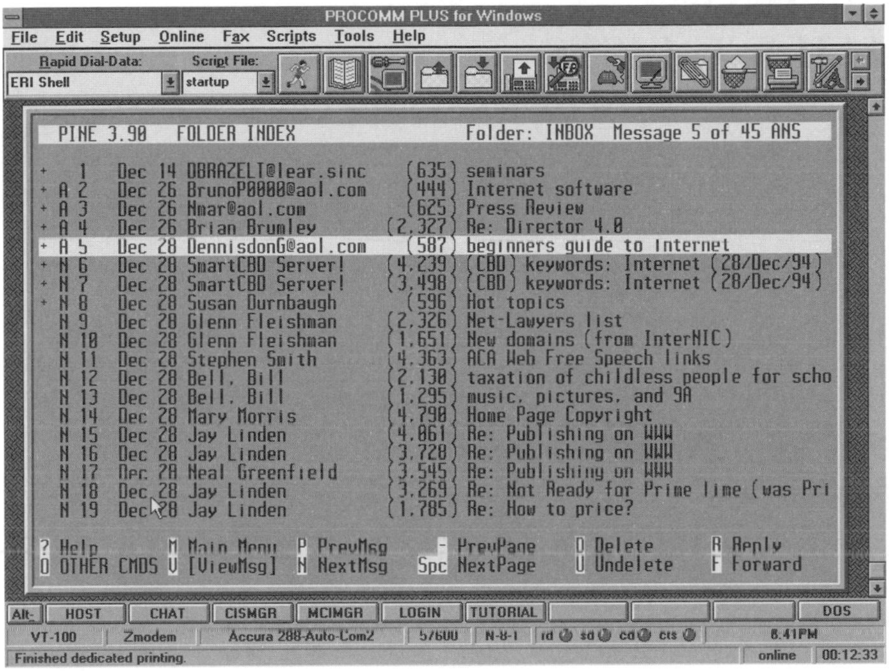

Figure 14-6

Don't forget to read the Frequently Asked Questions (FAQs) related to e-mail on your provider's system. Also, it's a good idea to browse through Pine's help screens to get to know the program's features and associated keystrokes.

Now that you know how to send and receive e-mail, let's move on to mailing lists which use e-mail as a medium for exchanging knowledge, ideas, and information.

CHAPTER 15
MAILING LISTS

BACKGROUND

The original intent of **mailing lists** was to provide a way for university professors and scientists to exchange ideas with one another on a one-to-many level, within distinct areas of discussion. The vehicle for message transmission remains e-mail.

As envisioned by the home of mailing lists, BITNET (the *Because It's Time Network)*, when one user wished to express views or information within a BITNET-based discussion topic, he joined (subscribed to) a mailing list set up for that topic. To join, he sent an e-mail message to the BITNET host address that managed administration for that topic.

HOW LISTS WORK

The one-to-many relationship is accomplished through the use of multiple distribution: when a user "subscribes" to a list, the system places his e-mail address in a database on a host server with others who also subscribe to that list. Then, whenever one user sends a note to the special "message submission" e-mail address for the topic, the list manager program sends a copy of that message to every subscriber of the list. So, as you can see, "automated" mailing lists use two different addresses (*administrative* and *message submission*), and the distinction between the two soon will be apparent.

Suppose that a group of educators and scientists wishes to share their thoughts and theories about the philosophy of technology. One of the nearly 7,000 mailing list topic areas is the "Philosophy and Technology" list, technically called PHTECH-L. To join the subscription list, each user sends a specially formatted e-mail message to an "administrative", automated e-mail address. Within a few minutes, he or she then receives a new e-mail message welcoming him or her to the list.

Shortly thereafter, the flow of e-mail messages from the PHTECH list begins, as users send e-mail to the list's "message submission" address. Subscribers read all, some, or none of the submissions, reply to them, or send new e-mail of their own. They can save, print, forward, or delete the messages.

LIST AUTOMATION

LISTSERV, the first component of the e-mail administrative address, is an automation program that subscribes users, unsubscribes users, and fulfills other online subscription chores.

LISTSERV receives e-mail requests and processes them automatically if the e-mail request is formatted properly. LISTSERV is one of a handful of list automation programs. Two other popular list maintenance programs are **MAJORDOMO** and **LISTPROC.** People often mistakenly refer to mailing lists as "listservs" because of the presence of the LISTSERV program.

A few mailing lists do not automate subscription activity. These mailing lists use normal e-mail addresses, and the administrative and submission functions sometimes use the same e-mail address. However, most lists are automated.

LIST SUBSCRIPTION ADDRESSING

As stated earlier, most mailing lists have two addresses associated with them. The first is the **administrative address** that potential subscribers cull from the name and location of the list. Returning to our example, the "Philosophy and Technology" list is formally called PHTECH-L. More completely, its title is PHTECH-L@PSUVM. PHTECH-L is the name of the list; PSUVM is the host site of the list. To subscribe to PHTECH-L, one restructures the PHTECH-L@PSUVM e-mail address to read `LISTSERV@PSUVM.BITNET` for mailing lists administered by Listserv.

Did you notice:

- *LISTSERV* was added as the first component of the address, to the left of @

- the -*L* part of the list name was dropped

- *PSUVM* was placed to the right of @

- *.BITNET* was added as the domain (we'll look at this in a moment)

PSEUDODOMAINS

Before going on, a word about the **pseudodomain** is in order. A *pseudodomain* is a quasi-domain that many Internet hosts recognize and honor. Pseudodomains sit at the end of an Internet address, are not one of the six U.S.-based domains, are not one of the international domains, and are longer than two or three letters. Where mailing lists are concerned, list subscribers may need to use the pseudodomain **.bitnet** in the administrative address (which you saw above: `LISTSERV@PSUVM.BITNET`. For those hosts that do not recognize pseudodomains, and there are a few, one must use a revised gateway address such as `LISTSERV%PSUVM@CUNYVM.CUNY.EDU` to reach the list's administrative address.

Did you notice that:

- *PSUVM* shifted to the left of the @ symbol

- a % sign was placed between LISTSERV and PSUVM

- the address *CUNYVM.CUNY.EDU* was added to help route the request

- the component *.BITNET* was dropped

SUBSCRIPTION FORMAT AND SYNTAX

At any rate, once you have determined which address to use, continue the subscription process by leaving the *Subject:* field blank, then by using one of the two following formats for the text body, typed exactly as you see here:

- If your list uses **LISTSERV:** SUBSCRIBE PHTECH-L FIRSTNAME LASTNAME See Figure 15-1.

- If your list uses **MAJORDOMO:** SUBSCRIBE PHTECH-L

Please note that since this is a common format, you can see the name of just about any automated list (GIGGLES@VTVM1 or WIN3-L@UICVM) and use this format to become a subscriber. Do not add or delete any words to this format, or it will not work!

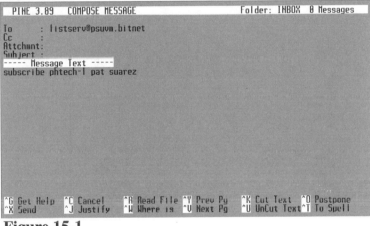

Figure 15-1

OTHER ADMINISTRATIVE ACTIVITIES

What else can you do with the administrative address? You can suspend message delivery without unsubscribing, see who else is on the list, and remove yourself from the subscription list. (See Appendix B)

USING THE LIST

Once the administrative program has accepted your subscription, you will begin to receive postings. Then, as the spirit moves you, either send a reply to someone else's posting or send a new one yourself. Some people go "off-list" to send personal replies via normal e-mail; others respond through the list itself. Reading the postings is as simple as reading new e-mail, because e-mail is how mailing lists send postings.

SUBMISSION ADDRESSING

The address to submit messages is, thankfully, easy. It is the official address name of the list you originally saw, as modified with a pseudodomain. For example, to submit your thoughts to the "Philosophy and Technology" list, use the e-mail address PHTECH-L@PSUVM.BITNET. See Figure 15-2. Remember the CUNY gateway if .BITNET is not accepted!

```
 PINE 3.89    COMPOSE MESSAGE                      Folder: INBOX   0 Messages

To      : phtech-l@psuvm.bitnet
Cc      :
Attchmnt:
Subject : Looking for comments
----- Message Text -----
Hello.

I am doing research on the positive and negative comments of
technological advances in communications as they relate to teens and the
problems teens face.

Please send your responses by private e-mail to pat@bgi.com.

Thank you.


Pat Suarez

^G Get Help  ^C Cancel     ^R Read File  ^Y Prev Pg   ^K Cut Text   ^O Postpone
^X Send      ^J Justify     ^W Where is  ^U Next Pg   ^U UnCut Text ^T To Spell
```

Figure 15-2

Some lists are **moderated;** that is, someone reads every potential posting before sending it to all list subscribers. The goal of moderating is to ensure that "off-subject" postings, messages having nothing to do with the topic of the list, are not sent to the list's subscribers.

On the other hand, most lists are **unmoderated,** and anything goes in unmoderated lists. Keep this in mind if your sensibilities are delicate or you can be provoked easily.

THE "LIST OF LISTS"

To get a list of most available mailing lists administered by LISTSERV (called the "list of lists"), create an e-mail message in the following format:

- To: LISTSERV@KSUVM.BITNET

- Subject: <blank>

- Text Body: list global

You will receive a 7,000-line response with the names of thousands of LISTSERV-administered mailing lists. Follow your communication software's instructions to either print the list or save it to a file (or both). Another way to find a list of your choice is to purchase an Internet "yellow pages" book, available at most bookstores. Once you have chosen a list, subscribe to it, read some postings, and send some of your own.

Another comprehensive, searchable source for mailing list (and newsgroup) names is the tutorial software, *The Beginner's Guide to the Internet,* available from Suarez Associates (pat@bgi.com).

A warning: Some lists generate over one hundred messages per day. Do not subscribe to too many mailing lists, or you may wind up with more messages than you can handle!

Also, when your subscription request is acknowledged, you should save the "welcome" e-mail message permanently because it will describe how to suspend service or unsubscribe from the list, something you will probably someday do.

CHAPTER 16
NEWSGROUPS

Another vehicle for posting messages in specific areas of interest is the **newsgroup,** a bulletin board system boasting approximately 12,000 topics that are forwarded by thousands of host systems. USENET was the first distributor of news articles in 1979.

The word "news" in the context of newsgroups means "articles", not news as defined as current events distributed by TV, radio, magazines, daily newspapers, and online services. However, special newsgroups exist that disseminate actual current event "news".

Newsgroups do not transmit messages via the e-mail system. Instead, host machines pass newsgroup postings to other machines that request them, and users employ special programs called **newsreaders** to access newsgroup topics, and read and post messages.

Newsgroups fall into one of several classes; Table 16-1 lists some of the most popular of them.

Each newsgroup class is broken into lower level hierarchies, as you will learn very shortly.

TABLE 16-1

alt	alternative subjects
bit	archives of BITNET mailing list traffic
biz	the world of business
ClariNet	"real" news-headlines, sports, weather, etc. *(not free!)*
comp	computers and computing
K12	the Internet and education
misc	miscellaneous discussions on a variety of topics
news	information about newsgroups
rec	recreational issues
sci	science and technology
soc	society and social issues
talk	debates about everything

Newsgroup topics are arranged in **hierarchies.** For example, under the top level newsgroup *rec.*(recreation) are dozens of immediate subtopics such as arts, aviation, sports, and others. Figure 16-1 shows a pictorial representation of the relationship among two levels of rec. newsgroup topic hierarchies. Notice that *rec.games* has two sublevels (*rec.games.trivia* and *rec.games.video*), while *rec.games.video* itself has two more levels of hierarchy (*rec.games.video.atari* and *rec.games.video.sega*). Keep in mind that each of these levels has postings from interested users. You can see why newsgroups occupy so much of the collective Internet resource total: there are nearly 12,000 newsgroups, and each can have hundreds of postings!

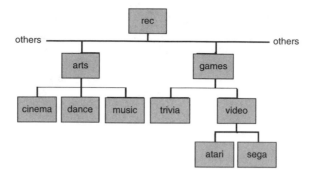

Figure 16-1

The most important distinction between mailing lists and newsgroups is that mailing list traffic comes to you automatically via e-mail if you subscribe. Newsgroup articles wait for you to come to them via a newsreader program installed as client software on your provider's host if you use the terminal emulation/Unix shell route or as Windows-based client software on your hard drive if you have TCP/IP capability.

All providers do not pass along every newsgroup. The two main reasons for this are **limited storage space** and **philosophy**.

All newsgroup traffic passed consumes hundreds of megabytes of storage each day. Smaller providers do not have the **storage capacity** to store and forward this kind of volume. Therefore, some providers offer a percentage of available news traffic. All providers remove and rotate articles from their servers after a short time, usually three to seven days. Users should consult with newsgroups of high interest to them frequently, lest potentially important announcements come and go unread.

The general volume of news articles has no effect on your computer if your access is through a dial-up; nothing lands permanently on your hard drive unless you actually download and store it there. Merely reading news articles with a newsreader does not fill your hard drive.

The other reason for limiting newsgroup access concerns **philosophy** and **censorship.** Many of the **alt** newsgroups are controversial, and organizations with no tolerance for their contents simply do not make them available, as is their right. However, if you are concerned about this limitation, you should sign on with a provider who has no problem with the contents of any newsgroup.

Several newsreader programs exist. The two most popular are **nn** and **tin.** The basic difference between them is that nn takes you directly into a newsgroup and displays a list of available messages, generally over several screens, while tin's screen lists several newsgroups over several screens, and you must select a newsgroup from the list to see the articles therein. A minor annoyance with tin is that it will list the title of a posting that was already deleted from the host system. Despite that, tin is easier to use than nn.

A newsreading session using *nn*:

1. At your provider's system prompt, type `nn`, then hit `<Enter>`. The system will prompt you for entry into a predetermined newsgroup such as `NEWS.NEWUSERS.QUESTIONS`. Hitting `<Enter>` will take you there. Ensure that your terminal emulation is set to *VT-100* if accessing `nn` or `tin` via a dial-up.

2. Alternatively, you may also type `nn` followed by a specific newsgroup name (`nn comp.os.msdos.apps`). If you do this, the newsreader will ask you to pick from a small menu of options (read all the postings, read just the postings you have not read, jump to a specific posting, and so forth). The most common selections are `a` for *all* or `u` for just the *unread* messages.

3. Once in a newsgroup, note the list of articles. Each has a letter next to it in the first column. The up and down arrows will cycle your cursor bar up and down through the list.

4. If the newsgroup postings cover more than screen, an inverse video bar at the bottom of the screen will display a percentage. This percentage represents how far through the postings you are at that screen. See Figure 16-2.

5. Find a posting that interests you, and type the corresponding letter (e.g., `e`).

6. Notice that an inverse video bar highlighted the posting line. (If you decide not to read the posting after having selected it, just hit the same letter, and the video bar will disappear.)

7. Hitting the space bar will take you through all the screens for the newsgroup. After you arrive at the final screen, hitting the space bar one more time will present the actual posting(s) you selected for you to read.

8. To go to another newsgroup, hit an upper case G, then type the new newsgroup's name. Select an option from the bottom of the screen for which postings you wish to read. See Figure 16-3.

9. To exit nn, type an upper case Q, then hit `<Enter>`.

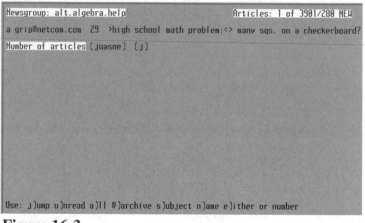

```
Newsgroup: comp.os.msdos.apps        Articles: 65 of 3901/288 UNSUB *NO*UPDATE*

a gary.salmond     16  ENVIRONMENT SPACE UNDER MS-DOS 6.XX
b David Tondreau   14  A source for PBASE
c Timo Salmi       88  Pointer to the combined FAQ of CBIP.wanted and CAM.d
d Timo Salmi       88  -
e Istvan Csiszar   37  SmartDrv...
f commafaq@alpha3  35  >>News and Mail FAQ: pointe<>comp.os.msdos.mail-news FAQs
g Pieter Hintjens  18  >filter for wfw6 to word for dos 6?
h Ben Schorr       17  Can put SCSI drive in IDE
i Mark Brabson     17  >How do you delete a h
j Mac McDougald    14  >>How to copy copy-protected 360K diskette to 720K?
k Mac McDougald     8  >>What is DOS 6.22. :)
l ZOGRAFAKIS       12  >>>
m I h g eyes       18  Orchid video card
n Hesham Elgharib  27  Data Entry automation. Need your help.
o Jan Just Keijser 23  >Copy music CD to hard-disk?
p Taka Torimoto    15  Where do I get something like K-Term?
q Frank Slootweg   11  >Program Groups Pass-portect (HELP)
r Jon Slater       33  DOS PPP setup
s Zhiyun Xie       12  Can msd detect modem device ?

-- 15:46 -- SELECT -- help:? -----Top 28%-----<level 2>--
```

Figure 16-2

```
Newsgroup: alt.algebra.help               Articles: 1 of 3901/288 NEW

a grip@netcom.com  29  >high school math problem:<> many sqs. on a checkerboard?

Number of articles (juasne) (j)




Use: j)ump u)nread a)ll @)archive s)ubject n)ame e)ither or number
```

Figure 16-3

A newsreading session using *tin*:

1. At your provider's system prompt, type tin, then hit <Enter>. The tin newsreader will attempt to "subscribe" you to all the new newsgroups which are not set to display in your tin session. You can select Y (Yes, add this newsgroup to my screen list), N (Do not add this newsgroup to my screen list but ask me about another one), or Q (Stop asking me to add new newsgroup names to my screen list and take me to my main tin screen). See Figure 16-4.

2. Select Q to go to your tin screen. You will see a list of presubscribed newsgroups, most of which have postings within them. You can select a newsgroup from that list; hit y (yank) to temporarily display every available newsgroup into your screen list–this could be up to 12,000 names!; or hit s to "subscribe" to another newsgroup. If you select s, tin will prompt you for the name of a newsgroup. Type it, then hit <Enter>. Once you subscribe to a particular newsgroup, its name will automatically appear on tin's newsgroup listing. See Figure 16-5. If there is a newsgroup name which you wish removed from your screen,

highlight it with your up/down arrow key, then select u to unsubscribe from it.

3.   You can also hit g to go directly to a newsgroup listed several screens down. To do that, select g, then type the name of the newsgroup to which you wish to go.

4.   Using the up/down arrow keys (or the space bar), highlight a newsgroup, then hit <Enter>.   The article list will appear. See Figure 16-6. It is likely that the topmost articles will actually be gone even though the article titles appear. To go to the first article with text in it, type the number 1, then hit <Enter>.   Tin will open the first posting it finds that contains data.

5.   Select a posting that is still in the system. If there is a string of replies to the original message, this is called a **thread.** You may read through the thread, or hit the left arrow key to leave the article and return to the menu.

6.   You may also use the forward slash key (/) to search for character strings that may be in the titles of the articles within each newsgroup. This is handy if you are looking for information in a sea of article titles. To do this, hit /, then enter a keyword at the ensuing prompt.

7.   You may mail an article to someone (even yourself!). Select an article title from the screen and hit m. Tin will prompt you for an e-mail address. Once you have entered that information, tin will e-mail the article across the Internet system.

8.   Selecting o will print a highlighted or current article.

9.   You may select w from the menu to post a new message to a newsgroup. Menu prompts along the way will lead you quickly through the process of creating and posting a new article to a newsgroup.

10. Select q to leave tin.

```
> tin
tin 1.2 PL2 [UNIX] (c) Copyright 1991-93 Iain Lea.
Reading news active file...
Subscribe to new group abe.business (y/n/q) [n]:
```

Figure 16-4

```
                    Group Selection (8963)                        h=help
    1     1    erinet.announce
    2          erinet.forsale
    3     8    erinet.internet
    4     4    erinet.local
    5          erinet.programmers
    6    58    erinet.support
    7          oh.cast
    8          oh.chem
    9   113    oh.general
   10          oh.k12
   11          oh.news
   12          oh.osc.software
   13     4    oh.test
   14     1    clari.apbl.biz.briefs
   15    53    clari.apbl.biz.headlines
   16    94    clari.apbl.briefs

    <n>=set current to n. TAB=next unread. /=search pattern. c)atchup.
  g)oto. j=line down. k=line up. h)elp. m)ove. q)uit. r=toggle all/unread.
    s)ubscribe. S)ub pattern. u)nsubscribe. U)nsub pattern. y)ank in/out

                        Added 8454 groups
```

Figure 16-5

```
            comp.internet.net-happenings (84T 85A 0K 0H R)         h=help
    1          JEWEL> GLOBAL News                      Gleason Sackman
    2    +     WWW> New Searchable Index of Recipes    Gleason Sackman
    3    +     HUNT> October Hunt Coming               Gleason Sackman
    4    +     WWW> New US-HIS Internet Resource        Gleason Sackman
    5    +     SOFT> HP3000 WWW server available        Gleason Sackman
    6    +     EMAG> Vibe Magazine - October issue available  Gleason Sackman
    7    +     MISC> New services on FedWorld BBS       Gleason Sackman
    8    +     MISC> NSF Announces Awards for Digital Librar  Gleason Sackman
    9    +     WWW> Memorex Telex WWW page              Gleason Sackman
   10    +     MISC> Internet Projects at Univ. Michigan  Gleason Sackman
   11    +     NEWSLTR> Cybernautics Digest            Gleason Sackman
   12    +     WWW> The Human-Language Page            Gleason Sackman
   13    +     WWW> LapLink Home Page                  Gleason Sackman
   14    +     WWW> MUD Pages on the Web               Gleason Sackman
   15    +     WWW> Center for Networked Multimedia    Gleason Sackman
   16    +     WWW> VIVA New Mexico!                   Gleason Sackman

    <n>=set current to n. TAB=next unread. /=search pattern. ^K)ill/select.
  a)uthor search. c)atchup. j=line down. k=line up. K=mark read. l)ist thread.
    |=pipe. m)ail. o=print. q)uit. r=toggle all/unread. s)ave. t)ag. w=post
```

Figure 16-6

One newsgroup that Internet newcomers should visit is
news.announce.newuser. This newsgroup contains newsgroup information useful to
Internet newcomers.

A final thought: Consider responding to a newsgroup posting via private e-mail,
especially if your comments would not anything substantial to the thread.

CHAPTER 17
TELNET (REMOTE LOGIN)

The ability to log into networks and host systems that are not connected to your computer (and may not even be in the same country you are in) is one of the Internet's key tools. This remote login feature is called **telnet.** You can use telnet with any Internet connection (e.g., dedicated line, PPP/SLIP access, terminal emulation dial-up, others). Because there may be several connecting points (called **hops**) between your computer and the remote system into which you wish to log, you may experience some delay from the time you press a keystroke to the execution of that keystroke. Note: As with several other Internet tools, nouns can be verbs. For example, you use telnet to remotely log into another network; this is also known as "telneting". Telnet is available as client software on most Internet host servers.

Before launching a telnet session, be aware of the following:

- When you use telnet to log into a remote host, you will see that system's main menu (if it has one), much like the menu you see when you log into a computer bulletin board system. At that point, you select a feature from the menu of the remote host, and you are off and running. *If you are using dial-up software through a modem, be sure that your terminal emulation setting is for* VT-100 *before telneting to a site!*

- There are two telnet operating modes, **input mode** and **command mode.** If your screen prompt looks like this: **telnet>** you are in *command mode*. Command mode allows you to configure your telnet session. For example, during your telnet session, if you press keys but the letters do not appear on the screen, typing `set echo` at the **telnet>** prompt in command mode will resolve the problem. *Input mode* is the normal telnet mode from your standard system prompt.

- During a telnet login, you must be aware of three pieces of information regarding your session:

- First, the **escape sequence**, which is usually ^] (control-right bracket). Sometimes, the escape sequence is ^\, but not often. In any event, always watch for the escape sequence during the login process. If you get stuck in the remote host and cannot exit from that system normally, using the escape sequence will blast you out of that remote host and back to either a command mode prompt or a standard input mode prompt. Please do not use the escape sequence as a substitute for the normal logout and exit procedure from the remote host!

- Second, the **login ID,** referred to on-screen as **login.** Sometimes, the remote host will tell you which login ID to use (e.g., `visitor`). If you are logging into a system to which you are already a member, use the login ID assigned to you by that system. This is handy for Delphi and CompuServe members who may wish to telnet to their accounts to check their e-mail there.

- Third, the **password.** Again, if you are logging into a system to which you are already a member, use your password for that system. If the system directs you to use a specific password, use it.

- Some systems impose a limit on the number of users that can be online at once, and this includes their own users at their site. You may be blocked from logging in because of overuse.

- If you cannot log in because `visitor` or `guest` logins are not honored by a remote system, you will have to call or write to plead your case for access authorization.

- Telnet addresses do not contain the @ symbol. In fact, only e-mail and Finger use addressing that contains the @ symbol.

- Some telnet addresses append a **port number** to the address (e.g., `madlab.sprl.umich.edu 3000`). The port number directs your login to a specific program on the server. Note the `<space>` before the port number.

Telnet gives you access to a wealth of information, from NBA schedules to government resources, from university libraries all around the world to freenets (local Internet BBS-like sites that charge nothing to belong to and that offer a host of options). Here are a few telnet sites to consider:

Hytelnet: Access Hytelnet from your prompt by typing `telnet access.usak.ca`. Hytelnet is Peter Scott's comprehensive catalog of telnet-accessible library sites. In all cases, Hytelnet explains what each site is and how to telnet to it; in some cases, you can telnet to a site from within Hytelnet's server menu.

Freenets: Freenets are local BBS-style resources available as either a dial-up for free in a city or via a telnet session. Universities often sponsor (pay for) the expenses associated with freenet operation.

Freenets offer telnet, e-mail, Gopher, file transfer protocol, and other Internet resources. The largest freenet is Case Western Reserve University's Cleveland Freenet, accessible via `telnet kanga.ins.cwru.edu`. See Figures 17-1 and 17-2.

Figure 17-1

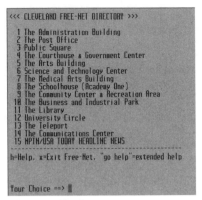

Figure 17-2

Online services: CompuServe and Delphi. You must be a paying member to these systems to telnet to them. If you are, use `telnet compuserve.com` and `telnet delphi.com`, respectively.

Sports schedules: There are several sports services. If you are a fan of the National Basketball Association or of one of its teams, find out what games are on tap using `telnet culine.colorado.edu 859`. Note the port number!

Free federal information: Take advantage of what your tax dollars pay for by using `telnet fedworld.doc.edu`. It is free and it is comprehensive.

A TELNET SESSION

1. At your system prompt, type `telnet locis.loc.gov`, then hit `<Enter>`. This is the telnet address for the Library of Congress. Note the escape sequence as it passes by. Also, remember that this entry was by way of *input mode*. You will arrive at a numbered menu, with the logout and exit at the bottom of the screen. See Figure 17-3.

2. Select the menu number of your choice and browse through the Library's contents. When you have finished, enter the logoff/exit keystrokes.

3. You should end up in input mode (at your main Internet prompt). If you find yourself in command mode (**telnet>**), type `quit`, then hit `<Enter>`.

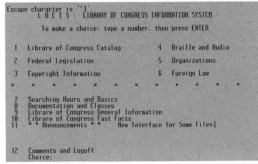

Figure 17-3

80

CHAPTER 18
FILE TRANSFER PROTOCOL (FTP)

File Transfer Protocol, or **ftp,** is similar to telnet in that it allows you to log into remote host systems. However, the hosts into which you log are special in that they act as servers that store and dispense files to other hosts. FTP is a complex subject that requires some familiarity with:

• file types

• file compression

• subdirectory structures

Let's begin with file types. Two types of files exist on ftp hosts, **ASCII** and **binary.** ASCII files, the most fundamental file type, are text files without special formatting or graphics, and usually have the filename extension of *.TXT* or *.DOC.* You can list the contents of an ASCII file on your computer screen or send those contents directly to most printers. Application programs, even those that employ proprietary file formatting (e.g., Microsoft Word for Windows), can read ASCII files.

Binary files fall into three general classes as set forth in Table 18-1.

TABLE 18-1

File Type	File Purpose	Typical Extension
Executable	Files that launch applications	.COM, .EXE
Graphic	Files that contain pictures or drawings	.GIF, .JPG
Compressed	Files that have been artificially reduced in size (number of bytes) and that might be made up of several files within a single file name	.ZIP, .ARJ, .ARC, .LHA, .z, .Z, .gz, .tar, .zoo

The distinction between the file types is important because packet transfers from router to router to host across the Internet are set for ASCII-type, not binary, data. Therefore, if you wish to transfer a binary file from one host to another, you must tell the system that the file you are about to transfer is indeed binary. If you do not alert the system that the file is binary, the system will consider the file to be ASCII and strip the eighth bit off each byte of binary data being transferred. The result will be a useless, trashed file. You will see how to set the file type to binary before transfer. Note: The default file type for transferring purposes is ASCII. If you wish to transfer an ASCII file, you do not have to establish the file type.

Some binary files may be configured to work with application programs that need specific operating systems (DOS, Unix, or Mac). So, if you have a file created on a Macintosh computer and you wish to use it on a DOS-based PC, you would have to try a "translation" program to see if it would convert.

File compression is technology that:

• reduces the amount of storage that a file takes up

• combines and shrinks several separate files within a single file name.

File compression is important because about 1,300 ftp hosts collectively store over two million files. Host managers "compress" most of the files on their host systems because space is often at a premium. For example, the size of the compressed file *BGI13A.ZIP* at the Oakland (MN) University ftp site is 97,368 bytes. But, it actually contains 19 files that, uncompressed, take up a total of 188,475 bytes. It is always up to the person downloading files from ftp sites to uncompress them.

THE ANONYMOUS LOGIN

Unlike telnet visits, which might require accounts on remote systems, most ftp sites allow **anonymous logins**. With anonymous logins, you do not need to be a registered user on the remote host, and the User ID/Login name is *anonymous* (literally); the Password is the user's e-mail address. For example, were the author of this textbook to login to an anonymous ftp site, the format would look like this:

User ID/Login: `anonymous`

Password: `pat@bgi.com` *(usually not echoed to the screen)*

This login format not only permits visitors to enter an ftp host but also enables the host to keep track of usage statistics (numbers of visitors, domain types, etc.). Note: Some ftp hosts, including some very popular ones, allow just 15 to 50 anonymous logins at a time. If a site rejects your anonymous login, it will usually list **mirror** sites that contain the same contents but may have more liberal anonymous login policies.

USING THE FTP COMMAND

To ftp to a site, simply type `ftp <site name>`, and hit `<Enter>`. The ftp site will then prompt you for a login ID and Password, as discussed above. An introductory screen, which the user should read, follows. Finally, the ftp prompt appears. It looks like this: **ftp>**. Note: The user may exit from the ftp process at any time by typing `quit`, then hitting `<Enter>`.

FTP SITE SUBDIRECTORY STRUCTURES

Many ftp sites employ several file storage subdirectories *and* several levels for each of those subdirectories. If you visit an ftp site just to browse, try to remember what level you are on and how that level relates to those above and below it. Note: You can always go up one level by typing `cd /`, then hitting `<Enter>`.

To pull up a list of the contents of a **current directory** (the directory where you are at that moment), type `ls -al`, then hit `<Enter>`. The ls -al command will produce a list of the contents of the subdirectory. Each line item has a string of letters and dashes called the **permission line**. Notice that some entries begin with **d**, while others begin with a dash (-).

The **d** indicates a subdirectory; the dash indicates a file. In Figure 18-1, *w8sdz* is the name of a subdirectory (with its own file and/or subdirectory structure). *README* is the name of a file that you could download to your computer. For filenames, other key data on the screen are:

• how big the file is, in bytes

• the date and time the file was created or last amended

```
ftp> ls -al
200 PORT command successful.
150 Opening ASCII mode data connection for /bin/ls.
total 1119
drwxrwxr-x  13 w8sdz     OAK         512 Oct  2 03:19 .
drwxrwxr-x  13 w8sdz     OAK         512 Oct  2 03:19 ..
-rw-r--r--   1 w8sdz     OAK           0 Aug 16  1992 .notar
-rw-r--r--   1 jeff      OAK     1120090 Oct  2 03:19 Index-byname
-r--r--r--   1 w8sdz     OAK        1439 Apr 26 11:56 README
drwxr-xr-x   2 w8sdz     OAK         512 Oct  1 10:40 SimTel
d--x--x--x   3 root      system      512 Aug 14 12:55 bin
d--x--x--x   2 root      system      512 Jul 30 18:54 core
drwxrwx---   2 cpm       OAK         512 Jul 30 22:29 cpm-incoming
d--x--x--x   5 root      system      512 Sep 18 20:59 etc
drwxrwx---   2 incoming  OAK         512 Oct  2 12:55 incoming
drwx------   2 root      OAK         512 Jan 10  1994 lost+found
drwxr-xr-x   6 w8sdz     OAK         512 Jul 30 20:10 pub
drwxr-xr-x  12 w8sdz     OAK         512 Jul 30 17:18 pub2
drwxr-xr-x   2 jeff      OAK         512 Apr 17 14:24 siteinfo
drwx------  27 w8sdz     OAK        1024 Oct  1 14:27 w8sdz
226 Transfer complete.
remote: -al
1001 bytes received in 1.4 seconds (0.71 Kbytes/s)
ftp>
```

Figure 18-1

FILE NAMING CONVENTIONS

Typically, there are two parts to file names under the IBM-based DOS operating system. The first is the **file name**, and it has a minimum length of one character and a maximum length of eight characters, with just a few special characters, but no spaces, allowed. The second part is the **file name extension**, which describes the file type, and has a character range of zero to three. Neither the file name or file name extension is **case-sensitive**, meaning the operating system makes no special distinction between upper and lower case letters. So, a legal DOS filename might be *WP.EXE* or *MYFILE.95*, but could be entered as *wp.exe* or *myfile.95*.

Unix is more flexible. Unix file names can be longer, with upper and lower case letters and special characters. *Unix file names are case sensitive!* So, the file name *My-Special_GIF_PhotoShot* is a legal name in Unix, but is unrecognizable to DOS.

Knowing these file naming conventions is important because you will encounter Unix files which you may want to download to your DOS-based computer. When you do, you will have to rename them before transferring them so that DOS can use them on your system.

FILE AND DIRECTORY RENAMING

Just as Unix files can have name structures foreign to DOS, so can directory names. If your Internet access is through a VMS or DOS environment (such as Delphi), use the following examples in Table 18-2 for directory and file renaming. As you will soon see, you do this renaming "on the fly" as you are processing. If your

Internet access is through a Unix host, the data in Table 18-2 does not apply!

TABLE 18-2

UNIX SUBDIRECTORY NAME	REVISED VMS/DOS NAME
cd New Files	cd "New Files"
UNIX FILE NAME	**REVISED VMS/DOS STRUCTURE**
get Club-member.list	get "Club-member.list" clublist.txt

Notes on Table 18-2:

- The Unix subdirectory name *New Files* contains a space, illegal in VMS/DOS. The VMS/DOS- corrected syntax encloses the subdirectory name in quotes and keeps its case structure. The command, cd "New Files", changes the current subdirectory name to something VMS and DOS can understand.

- The Unix file name *Club-member.list* is too long for VMS/DOS and has a file-name extension of more than three characters. To "get" (transfer) such a named file to a VMS or DOS system, first enclose the exact Unix file name in quotes, add one space, then create a legal file name and extension, without quotes. The command, get "Club-member.list" clublist.txt, changes the name of the file *Club-member.list* to *clublist.txt*, a name tolerable to VMS and DOS.

DIFFERENT INTERNET ACCESS METHODS AND FTP

File transfer using ftp is either a one-step or a two-step process, depending on how you are connected to the Internet. If you have a dedicated line or use either PPP or SLIP access, your computer is linked directly to the Internet backbone system by way of routers, and your computer has its own IP address. *When you use ftp, the file copies straight from the ftp host site to your hard drive.*

If you use terminal emulation to dial-up to a shell account and your computer does not have its own IP address, ftp is a two-step process. You first use the ftp command get to copy a file from the ftp host site to your Internet provider's host system (the one into which you dialed). Then, you must run *Zmodem protocol* to download the file from your provider's workspace to your hard drive. Most terminal emulation packages include the Zmodem program. Don't forget to erase the file from your provider's workspace after download!

FILE TRANSFER PROTOCOL SESSIONS

The ftp sessions in this chapter involve using the get command to copy files from ftp hosts to your computer. These session examples are specific to one of these scenarios:

- VT-100 dial-up through a Unix host

- VT-100 dial-up through a VMS host

85

Since so many different kinds of systems can access Internet services, one could generate dozens of scenarios specific to each. Because of the vast numbers of DOS-based computers that exist and because a large percentage of people use DOS-based machines (with and without Windows) calling into Unix hosts, the following examples are based on either DOS or Unix systems.

An ftp Session Using a VT-100 dial-up from a DOS machine to a Unix host

1. Dial up to a Unix host using a modem and VT-100 terminal emulation software.

2. Log into your system (login ID and Password) to a Unix prompt.

3. Type `ftp ftp.rpi.edu`, then hit `<Enter>`. (Note: Many ftp site addresses begin with the letters "ftp".)

4. At the login prompt, enter `anonymous`.

5. At the Password prompt, enter your Internet e-mail address.

6. Your prompt will change to **ftp>.** Type `ls -al`, then hit `<Enter>`. Notice the list of subdirectories (noted by the letter **d** in column one at the left edge of the screen) and files (noted by a dash <-> in column one at the left edge of the screen). If the list is longer than one screen, you may want to stop the scrolling to see part of the list. `^s` suspends screen scroll; `^q` resumes it.

7. Enter `cd pub`.

8. Enter `cd communications`[7.]

9. Enter `ls -al`. Since the list is longer than one screen, you may want to stop the scrolling to see part of the list. `^s` suspends screen scroll; `^q` resumes it.

10. You want to download the file `internet-cmc.txt`. Since this an ASCII text file, the ftp default, you do not have to establish the type.

11. However, the file name structure is foreign to DOS, so you will have to alter it so that DOS can read it. To transfer the file, enter the command: `get "internet-cmc.txt" cmc.txt`. This is the famous December List of Internet programs and protocols. See the bottom of Figure 18-2.

12. The file will transfer from the Rensselaer host to your Internet provider's host system—the system into which you dial.

13. Enter `quit` to leave ftp and return to your Unix system prompt.

14. To make the final transfer from your Internet provider's host to your computer, consult with your terminal emulation software to perform a Zmodem protocol download.

[7.]You could have entered `cd /pub/communications` on one line.

```
-rw-r--r--  1 12803       8883 Oct  4  1993 internet-cmc.gif
-rw-------  1 25504       2343 Aug 21 19:46 internet-cmc.html
-rw-------  1 25504     504846 Sep 19 02:39 internet-cmc.ps
-rw-------  1 25504     195379 Sep 19 02:39 internet-cmc.ps.2
-rw-------  1 25504      20775 Sep 19 02:39 internet-cmc.readme
-rw-------  1 25504     245831 Sep 19 02:39 internet-cmc.tex
-rw-------  1 25504       7147 Sep 19 02:39 internet-cmc.toc
-rw-------  1 25504     232871 Sep 19 02:39 internet-cmc.txt
-rw-------  1 25504       3495 Aug 21 19:46 internet-cmc.use
-rw-------  1 25504      76896 Sep 23 02:17 internet-tools
-rwx------  1 25504      64382 Sep 23 02:17 internet-tools.dat
-rw-------  1 25504     111304 Sep 23 02:17 internet-tools.dvi
-rw-r--r--  1 12803        303 Dec  1  1993 internet-tools.gif
-rw-r--r--  1 25504       2259 Jul 14 19:33 internet-tools.html
-rw-------  1 25504      74511 Sep 23 02:17 internet-tools.ps.2
-rw-------  1 25504       2282 Sep 23 02:17 internet-tools.readme
-rw-r--r--  1 12803       6924 Mar 12  1994 internet-tools.tax
-rw-------  1 25504      61214 Sep 23 02:17 internet-tools.tex
-rw-------  1 25504      62073 Sep 23 02:17 internet-tools.txt
-rw-------  1 25504      11417 Aug 21 19:08 internet-tools.use
226 ASCII Transfer complete.
remote: -al
1704 bytes received in 0.91 seconds (1.8 Kbytes/s)
ftp> get "internet-cmc.txt" cmc.txt
```

Figure 18-2

An ftp Session Using a VT-100 dial-up from a DOS machine to a provider using a VMS host to download a binary file:

1. Dial up to the VMS host using a modem and VT-100 terminal emulation software.

2. Log into your system (login ID and Password) to a VMS prompt.

3. Type `ftp oak.oakland.edu`, then hit `<Enter>`.

4. At the login prompt, enter `anonymous`.

5. At the Password prompt, enter your Internet e-mail address.

6. Your prompt will change to **ftp>.** Type `dir`, then hit `<Enter>`.
   Notice the list of subdirectories (noted by the letter **d** in column one at the left edge of the screen) and files (noted by a dash `<->` in column one at the left edge of the screen). Note: The `dir` and `ls -al` commands are interchangeable.

7. Enter `cd simtel/msdos/info`.

8. Enter `dir`. Since the list is longer than one screen, you may want to stop the scrolling to see part of the list. `^s` suspends screen scroll; `^q` resumes it.

9. You want to download the file `bgi20.zip`. Since this a binary file, not an ASCII text file, the ftp default, you must establish the type. Do so by entering `binary` at the VMS prompt.

10. To transfer the file, enter the command `get bgi20.zip`.

11. The file will transfer from the Oakland University host to your Internet provider's host system—the system into which you dial. See Figure 18-3.

12. Enter `quit` to leave ftp and return to your VMS system prompt.

13. To make the final transfer from your Internet provider's host to your computer, consult with your terminal emulation software to perform a Zmodem protocol download.

```
ftp> binary
200 Type set to I.
ftp> get bgi20.zip
200 PORT command successful.
150 Opening BINARY mode data connection for bgi20.zip (384216 bytes).
226 Transfer complete.
local: bgi20.zip remote: bgi20.zip
384216 bytes received in 29 seconds (13 Kbytes/s)
ftp>
```

Figure 18-3

ARCHIE

There are over two million files stored on over 1,300 ftp sites around the world. A program called **Archie** maintains an index of the file names at those sites, and you can search through that index to find a file. Archie updates all of them within a 30-day cycle, exploring 1/30 of the sites each day.

You can access Archie as client software or telnet to it. There are occasional problems with the Archie system, mostly related to its popularity. First, Archie hosts can be hard to reach, but persistence will pay off as users log on and off throughout the day. Second, some Archie servers quickly time-out and discontinue a search. Third, users are encouraged to log into the Archie server nearest to them, geographically. Two friendly Archie telnet sites are **archie.rutgers.edu** and **archie.internic.net.**

You can configure your Archie session once you have reached an Archie prompt (**archie>**). For example, it is a good idea to use the command `set maxhits 10` at the prompt because the file you are trying to find might be on dozens of ftp hosts and you rarely need to see a list of every host storing the same file. The default number of hits is 95.

The default configuration for filename searching is sub, which means that you can type part of a filename (`pkz` for `pkz204g.zip,` for example). If you want Archie to search for only exact character strings, use the command `set exact` at the **archie>** prompt, but this reduces Archie's flexibility.

An Archie Session:

1. Log into an Internet session.

2. At your Internet prompt, type `telnet archie.internic.net.`

3. At the login prompt, enter `archie`.

4. If that site is busy and refuses logins, consult the list of alternate sites that Archie will present, and try one of those.

5. You will see the Archie prompt: **archie>.** At the prompt, enter `set max-hits 10`.

6. Enter `prog pkz`. See Figure 18-4.

7. Shortly, you will see a list of ftp sites above the subdirectory pathnames for all the files found. The filenames will be to the right of the pathnames. See Figure 18-5. Note the results, which will point you to the proper ftp server, subdirectory, and file name.

8. Enter `quit` to leave Archie.

```
login: archie

************************************************************************

             Welcome to the InterNIC Directory and Database Server.

************************************************************************


* Bunyip Information Systems, 1993

* Terminal type set to 'vt100 24 80'.
* 'erase' character is '^?'.
* 'search' (type string) has the value 'sub'.
archie> set maxhits 10
archie> prog pkz
```

Figure 18-4

```
Host freebsd.cdrom.com    (192.216.222.5)
Last updated 06:11 23 Sep 1994

    Location: /.2/SimTel/msdos/zip
        FILE   -r--r--r--  282574 bytes  01:00 17 Jan 1993  pkz204g.exe

    Location: /.3/garbo/pc/arcers
        FILE   -r--r--r--  282574 bytes  01:00 31 Jan 1993  pkz204g.exe


Host hpcsos.col.hp.com    (15.255.240.16)
Last updated 10:00 21 Sep 1994

    Location: /hamradio/packet/n6gn/uwavelink/pcb
        FILE   -rw-r--r--  282574 bytes  00:00 24 May 1993  pkz204g.exe

    Location: /hamradio/packet/wa7tas
        FILE   -rw-r--r--  282574 bytes  01:00 15 Mar 1993  pkz204g.exe


Host ftp.halcyon.com    (198.137.231.11)
Last updated 09:43 21 Sep 1994

:
```

Figure 18-5

89

CHAPTER 19

GOPHER

Gopher is a menu-driven tool that leads you to a wealth of files and information. When you enter a Gopher session, you actually use the resources of some remote host system tuned to respond to Gopher commands.

You can Gopher from host to host seamlessly. Gophering might appear to be just a menu change to you, but a menu choice might send you to a system on another continent to perform a telnet session or across the state for an ftp session. This flexibility exists because the underpinnings of Gopher point to routines that use telnet, ftp, white-pages servers, library systems, electronic bulletin board systems, and other communication tools.

Gopher is available as client software on most Internet provider hosts. You access it by just typing the word `gopher` at your Unix shell prompt, and you will log into a Gopher server elsewhere.

If Gopher is unavailable as client software on your provider's host, you may telnet to a Gopher. The telnet address is `consultant.micro.umn.edu`; the login is `gopher`. You will rarely have to telnet to use Gopher, however.

Assuming that Gopher is available as client software on your provider's host, just entering `gopher` at your Internet prompt will take you (virtually) to the home of the original Gopher, the University of Minnesota.

You may also Gopher to a specific Gopher server. To do that, use the following syntax at your Internet prompt: `gopher <gopher address>`. For example, to visit the informative Gopher at InterNIC, enter this at your Internet shell prompt: `gopher gopher.internic.net`.

There are thousands of Gopher servers around the world, and you can get to most of them, eventually, by selecting menu item after menu item. If you find a Gopher server you like, you may have traversed half a dozen levels or more. But, your system can "memorize" the path and keep a list of favorite Gopher sites. The list is called a Gopher **bookmark.**

To use the Gopher bookmark, type the letter a when you are at a Gopher site you wish to save. A confirming dialog box will appear on the screen; hit `<Enter>` to record the site into your bookmark list. Thereafter, when you are in a Gopher session, type the letter v to call up your bookmark list.

Note: If you access Gopher via a terminal emulation dial-up, set your emulation to VT-100. Also, note the menu items at bottom of the Gopher screen. Pressing the u key takes you backward through the Gopher menu selections you have traveled during your Gopher session; the left arrow key has the same effect.

A Gopher Session:

1. Log onto an Internet session.

2. At Unix prompt, enter `gopher`.

3. The Gopher client program will take you to the University of Minnesota Gopher host.

4. Study the menu. Item 8 will take you to thousands of other Gopher hosts worldwide. Item 8 also contains the *Veronica* search tool, which is the next subject in this chapter. At this point, select any menu item you wish and just roam. Remember that either u or the left arrow key will take you back one menu level.

5. Menu items that end with a forward slash (/) have more menu items under them. Menu items that end with <?> ask for a word to start some sort of search. When you encounter text data, the bottom of the screen will offer action options such as mailing, saving, and printing. Keep in mind that if you are at a public Gopher, some of these options might not be available to you. See Figure 19-1.

6. If you find a Gopher site that you want to enter as a bookmark for a return visit, hit the a key, then respond to the confirming dialog box that will appear on the screen.

7. Hit q to leave Gopher.

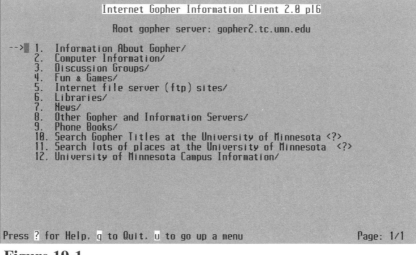

Figure 19-1

Veronica is a search device that maintains a constantly-updated index of the Gopher menus and locates information based on keywords. Veronica is a Gopher menu item, typically under *Other Gopher and Information Services*, or some similarly titled menu item.

A Veronica Session:

1. Log into a Gopher session.

2. Select appropriate menu items until you reach a Veronica menu item, then select it. See Figure 19-2.

3. A list of Veronica sites will appear. Select the one geographically closest to you. If it is busy, pick an alternate site. See Figure 19-3.

4. A dialog box will appear on the screen. Type a keyword such as `music`, then hit `<Enter>`. See Figure 19-4. *Always be aware of any possible menu choices that are on the screen.*

5. Shortly, a list of responses will appear. Select one or more to see what Veronica found. Keep in mind that, at times, Veronica will list a reference site to which you will not be granted access. See Figure 19-5.

6. Log off your Gopher session.

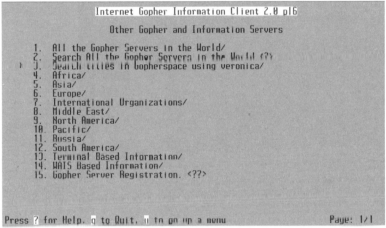

Figure 19-2

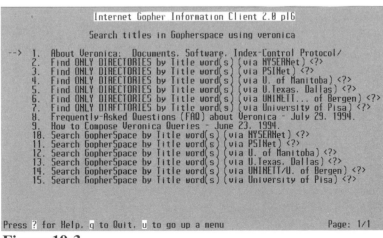

Figure 19-3

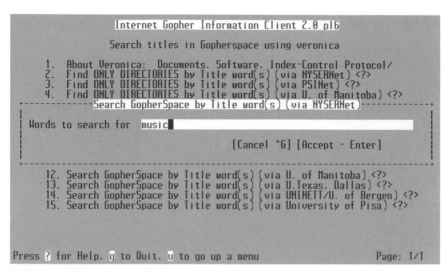

Figure 19-4

```
         Internet Gopher Information Client 2.0 pl6
        Search GopherSpace by Title word(s) (via NYSERNet): music

-->  1.  music.
     2.  music.
     3.  Music Cataloguing for Nonspecialist.
     4.  Music Materials in Libraries.
     5.  Music Cataloguing for Nonspecialist.
     6.  Music Materials in Libraries.
     7.  Medieval & Renaissance Music.
     8.  Multimedia Music Project.
     9.  Music/
    10.  Music Archives (Univ. Wisconsin-Parkside)/
    11.  Music.txt.
    12.  Music.
    13.  Music/
    14.  music_Deep-Purple-faq_Part.
    15.  music_Deep-Purple-faq_part1.
    16.  music_Deep-Purple-faq_part2.
    17.  music_acappella-faq_PartOne.
    18.  music_acappella-faq_PartThree.
Press ? for Help. q to Quit. u to go up a menu          Page: 1/12
```

Figure 19-5

94

CHAPTER 20

WIDE AREA INFORMATION SERVER (WAIS)

The Wide Area Information Server **(WAIS)** maintains indexes of the *contents* of documents on hundreds of WAIS servers around the world. This is in contrast to Veronica, which indexes Gopher server menu data, not the contents of the Gopher data itself. Also, to further the distinction, WAIS information is stored in WAIS servers, not Gopher servers.

You can access WAIS from telnet, Gopher, and through Mosaic. As with other Internet tools, you can access WAIS via client software on your provider's system, if offered. Hint: The fastest, cleanest WAIS access is through Gopher. WAIS through telnet or client software can present some frustrations because of occasional, unpredictable VT-100 emulation behavior and line delays. The best advice is to access WAIS through Gopher.

Some WAIS basics:

1. Look over the WAIS server topic list which consists of about 500 entries,

2. Highlight the name of the server you wish to search,

3. Enter a keyword,

4. Wait for the results.

WAIS ranks and scores the results of a search. A search result score accompanies each search result item, with the best score possible equaling 1000. WAIS calculates search scores based on the number of times the keyword appears in the documents, the length of the documents, and a few other factors. Lower-score 'hits" are based on the documents which received the score of 1000. You can print or e-mail the results of a search. If you accessed WAIS through client software, you can save the screen output to a file on your system.

WAIS searches are not sophisticated. You cannot use AND, OR, or NOT to define a search, nor can you use the * wildcard character. Also, you may encounter inaccessible hosts when trying to search for information. If that happens, try again later.

A WAIS Session:

1. Start a Gopher session.

2. At the main Gopher menu, select **Other Gopher and Information Servers.**

3. Select the WAIS menu item. See Figures 20-1 and 20-2.

4. A list of WAIS resources will appear as a multi-screen menu.

5. The next step is to search for the title of an appropriate WAIS server. To do that, hit the forward slash key (/), then enter a keyword in the ensuing dialog box. In this example, that keyword is `zipcodes`. See Figure 20-3.

6. Gopher will locate and select the *zipcodes* server title.

7. With the zipcodes resource selected, hit the / key to enter bring up a dialog box to enter a keyword. Type the character string 45343, and hit <Enter>. See Figure 20-4.

8. After a few seconds, WAIS will report back that *45343* belongs to *Miamisburg, Ohio*. Note: You could have searched on the word *Miamisburg* and found *45343*, as well. See Figure 20-5.

9. Hit q to quit WAIS.

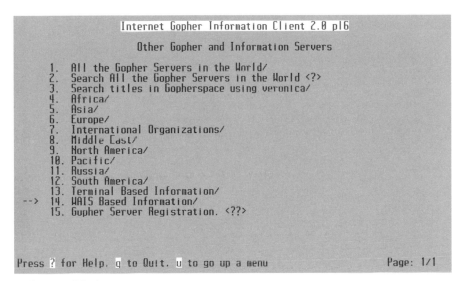

Figure 20-1

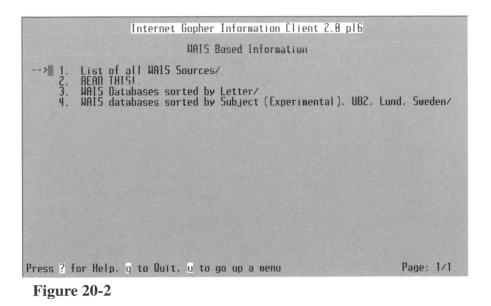

Figure 20-2

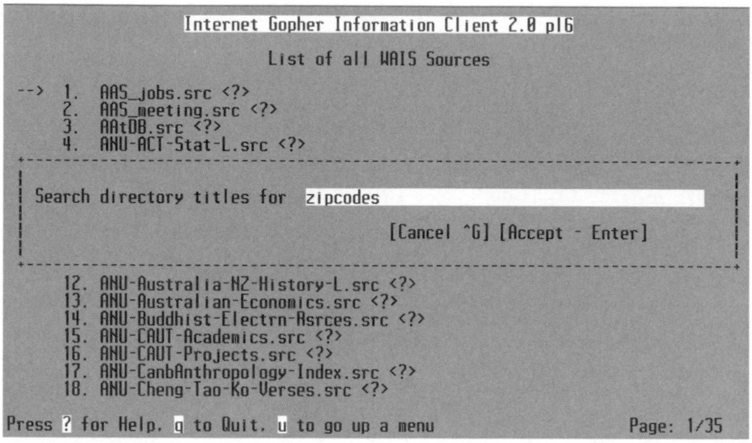

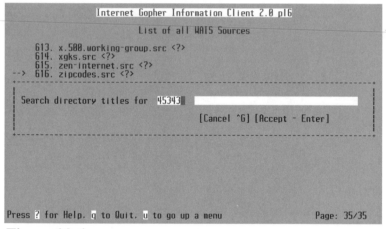

Internet Gopher Information Client 2.0 pl6
List of all WAIS Sources
--> 1. AAS_jobs.src <?>
2. AAS_meeting.src <?>
3. AAtDB.src <?>
4. ANU-ACT-Stat-L.src <?>
Search directory titles for zipcodes
[Cancel ^G] [Accept - Enter]
12. ANU-Australia-NZ-History-L.src <?>
13. ANU-Australian-Economics.src <?>
14. ANU-Buddhist-Electrn-Rsrces.src <?>
15. ANU-CAUT-Academics.src <?>
16. ANU-CAUT-Projects.src <?>
17. ANU-CanbAnthropology-Index.src <?>
18. ANU-Cheng-Tao-Ko-Verses.src <?>
Press ? for Help, q to Quit, u to go up a menu
Page: 1/35

Figure 20-3

Internet Gopher Information Client 2.0 pl6
List of all WAIS Sources
613. x.500.working-group.src <?>
614. xgks.src <?>
615. zen-internet.src <?>
--> 616. zipcodes.src <?>
Search directory titles for 45343
[Cancel ^G] [Accept - Enter]
Press ? for Help, q to Quit, u to go up a menu
Page: 35/35

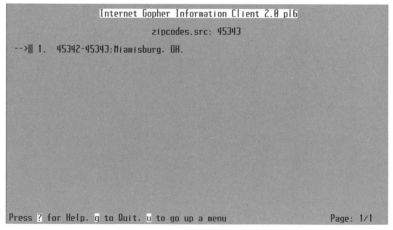

Figure 20-4

Internet Gopher Information Client 2.0 pl6
zipcodes.src: 45343
--> 1. 45342-45343:Miamisburg, OH.
Press ? for Help, q to Quit, u to go up a menu
Page: 1/1

Figure 20-5

CHAPTER 21
FINDING PEOPLE

The most foolproof way of getting a person's e-mail address is to ask that person what it is. But, the Internet has made great strides in developing a white pages directory of as many people as possible. One roadblock is that many networks do not release their user lists to the general public.

But if you want to be listed, you can be. The quickest way to get your own listing is to call InterNIC at 619-455-4600. InterNIC will guide you through the steps to become listed so that anyone can locate your Internet e-mail address.

Programs such as Whois and Netfind maintain databases of users, but a more comprehensive program is **Knowbot** which searches several white pages databases but does not maintain any data itself. You reach Knowbot through telnet.

A Knowbot Session:

1. Log into an Internet session.

2. Enter `telnet info.cnri.reston.va.us 185`.

3. When prompted, enter your Internet e-mail address.

4. At the Knowbot prompt (>), enter part or all of a name of your choice. The example in Figure 21-1 is `suarez`. Shortly, Knowbot will report the results after searching several databases. See Figure 21-2.

5. Note the results, then enter `quit` to exit Knowbot.

```
> telnet info.cnri.reston.va.us 185
Trying 132.151.1.15 ...
Connected to info.cnri.reston.va.us.
Escape character is '^]'.

                Knowbot Information Service
KIS Client (V2.0).    Copyright CNRI 1990.    All Rights Reserved.


KIS searches various Internet directory services
to find someone's street address, email address and phone number.

Type 'man' at the prompt for a complete reference with examples.
Type 'help' for a quick reference to commands.
Type 'news' for information about recent changes.

Backspace characters are '^H' or DEL

Please enter your email address in our guest book...
(Your email address?) > pat@bgi.com

> suarez
```

Figure 21-1

100

```
The rs.internic.net whois server is being queried:

Suarez Associates (BGI-DOM)                                             BGI.COM
Suarez Corporation Industries (COMPCLUB-DOM)                       COMPCLUB.COM
Suarez, Carlos (CS359)                                           (202) 623-1205
Suarez, Pat (PS81)                          pat@BGI.COM          (513) 323-6121
Suarez, Philip (PS87)                       philip@ICSI.NET
                                               (512) 572-9987 (FAX) (512) 572-8193
Suarez, William (WS52)                      Suarez@DIGPROD.COM   (617) 647-1234 X-221

The nic.ddn.mil whois server is being queried:

Suarez, Antonette A. (AAS31)                     (310) 795-2230 (DSN) 972-2230
Suarez, Carlos (CS359)                                          (202) 623-1205
Suarez, Carlos E. (CE571)       SUAREZC@LEE-EMH2.ARMY.MIL
                                            (804) 734 7942 (DSN) 687-7942
Suarez, Donald A. A. (DAS76)    mbsuarez@TECNET1.JCTE.JCS.MIL
                                318 456-2518 (DSN) 781-2518 (FAX) 318 456-2638
Suarez, Epinenio, ATRRS (ES271) SP221@PENTAGON-GW1.ARMY.MIL      210-625-6772
(Press RETURN to continue)█
```

Figure 21-2

USING FINGER

Finger is a clever program that:

• returns information on users registered to Unix systems.

• tells who is logged on to a system at any given time.

• automatically returns text and information.

Entering `finger user@host.site.domain` will return information about that user if the system's manager "enabled" finger access.

Entering `finger @host.site.domain` at your Unix prompt will show who is logged on to that system if the system's manager "enabled" finger access.

Some host system managers turn Finger "off" so that information about users is unavailable. Finger is famous for keeping track of the contents of a soda pop machine in Australia. Something to try: At your Internet prompt, enter `finger info@nttc.com`. Finger will return information on how the various Internet tools that dispense all you need to know about the National Technology Transfer Center in West Virginia.

101

CHAPTER 22
THE WORLD WIDE WEB

Nothing has created more of a sensation in the world of the Internet than the **World Wide Web**. Until early 1993, the Web was a just clever way to access information because it employed two programming devices. First, the Web was a **hypertext** vehicle. Upon opening a Web session under VT-100 emulation, the user saw that certain words or phrases were marked by numbers in brackets and highlighted in inverse video. When the user moved the screen cursor block from highlighted word to highlighted word, or when he selected a number entry from the screen, then hit the Enter key, new words or documents appeared on the screen because they were *linked* to the word or phrase he had selected. The user could hypertext his way through a seemingly endless succession of links and screens.

Second, the Web hypertext system had some elaborate underpinnings. Within the Web's links were embedded ftp, Gopher, telnet, e-mail, WAIS, and other Internet tools. So, the Web was much more than a text-reading device.

The first Web interface, called the *line mode browser*, did not do the Web justice. A more sophisticated front end called **Lynx,** developed at the University of Kansas, offered a menu along with the hypertext features. See Figure 22-1. The chief benefit of Lynx was the ability to call upon Web, Gopher, or ftp sites directly by using the keystroke g. When the user arrived at a destination, the forward slash (/) enabled searches from within that resource. Lynx remains a quick and powerful text-based browser. However, Lynx has been all but upstaged by a virtual Internet revolution called **Mosaic.** We will examine it and other graphical Web browsers in detail in Part 3.

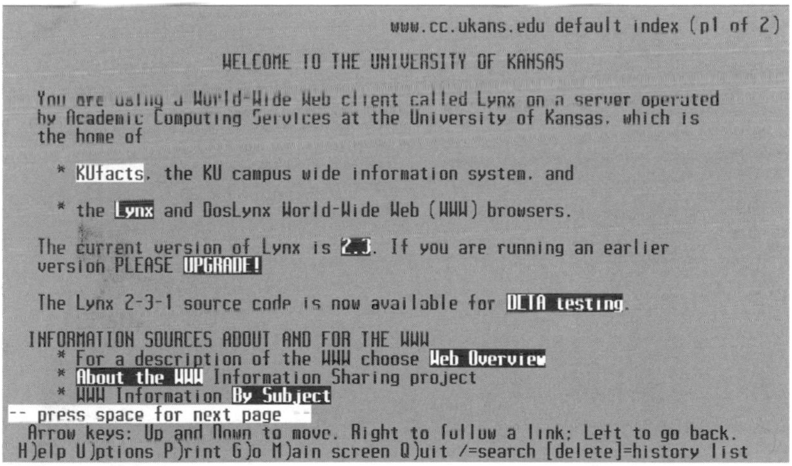

Figure 22-1

The Web uses the **URL,** Universal Resource Locator, to load Web, ftp, Gopher, and other documents and host menus. Examples of URL addressing are: *http://www.npr.org/* or *http://www.internic.net/htbin/search-net-happenings* **http** stands for hypertext transfer protocol, the standard for Web documents. Notice that there are no spaces in an http URL.

ftp://oak.oakland.edu As you can see, you can use ftp from within the World Wide Web. Graphical Web browsers (Netscape, Mosaic, and the rest) allow you to point and click your way through ftp host subdirectories.

gopher://gopher.internic.net Again, the Web makes a text-based application easy, although it's pretty hard to make Gopher menuing much easier than it already is.

telnet://dayton.wright.edu Telnet sessions open a telnet client program, such as NetManage's TELNET.EXE, and process remote logins from within Microsoft Windows.

The implication is that the World Wide Web, especially through its graphical browsers, is becoming the focal point for nearly every Internet tool. Netscape can process Web, Gopher, ftp, WAIS, telnet, and newsgroup[8] sessions.

Graphical Web browsers used to be the exclusive province of those with PPP, SLIP, or dedicated access. Not anymore. Cyberspace Development markets *The Internet Adapter*, software that allows Unix shell dial-up customers to have a temporary SLIP connection to the Internet backbone so that Netscape or Mosaic will work.

Here's how TIA works:

1. Your Internet provider installs TIA on his host server.

2. You start Windows on your computer.

3. You load a WINSOCK compliant TCP/IP program such as Trumpet Winsock to your screen.

4. You log into a "virtual" (simulated) SLIP session from your TCP/IP program. Note: Understanding this can be a bit tricky. Although your PC performs actions that any SLIP connection would allow (direct ftp service from an ftp host right to your PC, for example), your PC cannot have its own Internet address/identity and cannot be a true host directly tied to the Internet routers and backbones. That is why this is a "virtual" SLIP session. You can do things that people with SLIP accounts can do, except for having true host status for your PC.

5. Once logged on, you load Netscape, Mosaic, Winweb, or other Web browser and use it as if you had dialed into a PPP or SLIP session.

   An added bonus for TIA users is that ftp transfers will go directly to their hard drives even though they have shell accounts!

TIA is software that your Internet service provider installs to his host server. Another option that shell account users have to open simulated (virtual) SLIP sessions is through client software that users install on their hard drives: MicroMind's shareware program called *Slipknot*.

---

[8]Netscape has one of the most powerful newsreaders in the industry embedded into it.

Slipknot gives shell account users virtual SLIP connections, and so users can use graphical Web browsers as if they had the more sophisticated SLIP hookups. To reiterate, TIA and Slipknot give the shell account user the same result, a virtual SLIP connection, but the former loads downstream on the host server, while Slipknot is software for the user's hard drive.

You may obtain Slipknot via ftp at `interport.net`. Go through the `pub`, `pbrooks`, and `slipknot` subdirectories to locate the compressed file that holds the Slipknot software.

Who would need TIA or Slipknot?

Users whose Internet provider charges more than about $30 per month for a PPP or SLIP connection, but offer shell accounts for $30 or less per month could use either. Slipknot is an attractive alternative if your provider is not inclined to load TIA on to his system.

But, if your provider offers PPP or SLIP connections for $30 or less per month, go with that and skip TIA and Slipknot.

Also, there are some users who only have access to shell accounts. For them. Slipknot (especially) is just what the virtual doctor ordered.

CHAPTER 23
INTERNET RELAY CHAT

Internet Relay Chat, or IRC, lets people "talk" live to one another using the keyboard and monitor. During an IRC session, whatever you type and enter shows up on the screens of others connected with you. IRC is normally client software on your Internet provider's host server.

To use IRC:

1. Log into a Unix shell session.

2. At the Unix prompt, enter `IRC`.

3. At the ensuing prompt, enter `/list` to list the current chat areas . There may hundreds of chat areas open concurrently.

4. When you see a chat subject you like, enter `/join <#chat_area>`. Don't forget the # symbol. Also, consider using an "alias" instead of your real name if the chat area is controversial and you intend to mix things up. If you need help, enter `/help`.

5. When you want to quit, enter `/quit`.

For the shell account user, your Internet provider loads IRC client software on his host server. When you begin an IRC session from a shell account, the provider's IRC software locates a host somewhere that offers itself up as a gateway for global IRC chatting and hooks you to it. Many host computers offer their services as IRC gateways, and your provider usually predetermines which server will be selected for your IRC session.

The PPP and SLIP customer must, of course, use his/her own IRC client software. This means that he or she must also select an IRC server when he or she invokes his/her IRC client program. Configuring Windows based IRC client software can be tricky, so all users might want to consult their providers for some assistance.

PART 3

The Internet via PPP/SLIP and Microsoft Windows

CHAPTER 24

ACCESSING THE INTERNET GRAPHI-CALLY

You learned in Part 1 that you could establish an Internet identity on your own computer through special Windows-based software and a PPP or SLIP connection through your Internet provider. Part 3 demonstrates how to use these tools. The examples come from the NetManage Chameleon software suite that contains

• TCP/IP software and its attendant WINSOCK.DLL driver

• Application client software for e-mail, ftp, and so on

It might be helpful to glance at the hardware requirements set forth in Chapter 8. You will also need Microsoft Windows (Windows for Workgroups is actually preferable) and the Chameleon package. A bonus: Much of the shareware and freeware that is available for use with Windows-based Internet access is "Winsock-compliant", which means that you can use it in lieu of the applications included in Chameleon or Internet-In-a-Box, and you just might want to.

None of the current "suites" is faultless. For example, the e-mail program from Internet-In-a-Box has a reply feature problem that makes it the last choice among all mail programs[9].

Here's a recommendation right from the start: If you have to use just one graphical Web browser, choose Netscape, not Mosaic.

Netscape and Mosaic "cache" the graphical images they display; that is, they create a record of them in a subdirectory on your hard drive. Here's why that's a big deal: Suppose you access a site with graphic images that don't change, and these graphic images take a minute or so to bring across the Internet routers and draw on your screen. The next time you access that site, Netscape will check to see if it has cached this site on your hard drive. If so, it will take the image from the hard drive instead of dragging it in over again from the server that holds the image data.

Another plus in Netscape's favor: More and more Web home pages have forms that look for Netscape because the creators of those forms designed them with Netscape in mind.

There are other Web browsers, and we'll examine them later.

An interesting note: NetManage's Chameleon product line did not include a home grown Web browser, and Spry made much of this with its AirMosaic that it included with Internet-In-a-Box.

---

[9] The problem is esoteric, but significant. When you wish to reply to mail you've just read, you can pull the "read" message into your reply, as you can in Pine and Chameleon Mail. But, I-Box encloses the message to which you are replying with horizontal lines at the top and bottom of that message. It does not precede each line with the > symbol, so recipients will have a hard time distinguishing the original message from your reply.

Now, NetManage offers a Web browser called the WebSurfer. Like Netscape, it also caches images, and it has a unique feature that is useful to those who program Web home pages; it allows the user to tinker with the makeup of Web pages. Most users won't need this feature, but NetManage markets flexible, powerful products sometimes geared to the more sophisticated user.

SOMETHING TO KEEP IN MIND

Do not confuse using Windows based TCP/IP software to access the Internet directly (through a PPP or SLIP connection) with using Windows based terminal emulation software to access a host server to put yourself in a Unix shell session that is indirect. You might be using Windows based application software, but you should now know (and not forget) that the two sessions are as different as night and day; one is direct to the backbones and the other simply makes your computer a terminal on a server.

You will notice...

Throughout the following subchapters, you will not see a lot of narrative.

This is because:

- You have already learned the concepts behind the activities. You are now merely putting them into play in a point and click environment.

- The Windows based tools are very easy to use, far easier than Unix based tools. In most cases, even the Windows neophyte will be able to grasp how these programs work; they really are that intuitive!

CHAPTER 25
LOADING CHAMELEON

Among the handful of competing TCP/IP programs available, your author selected NetManage's Chameleon because:

- it is a stable, mature product.

- it has a comprehensive selection of client applications.

- its TCP/IP program works with third party, Winsock compliant Windows applications such as PCEudora and WinFTP.

- it is easy to set up: one menu bar item establishes the Internet based configuration while a second handles modem connections.

- it comes in three flavors:

  - A free sampler with small TCP/IP application suite.

  - A lower-priced complete TCP/IP application package called *Internet Chameleon*.

  - A top-of-the-line deluxe TCP/IP application package called Chameleon. Note: Chameleon is a full-blown networking product that includes TCP/IP Internet access.

What you need to do now is to load Windows and locate the Chameleon program group....

Find the Chameleon program group, double-click to open it, and examine its application icons. See Figure 25-1. Each application tool (e-mail, Gopher, and so on) has its own icon which you double-click to open.

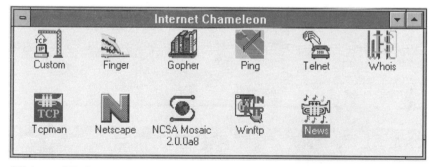

Figure 25-1

Note in Figure 25-1 that the bottom row of icons (Tcpman, Mosaic, Netscape, Winftp, and News) are not part of the Chameleon package but were added manually. Note also that the numbers of available client programs (and, therefore, icons) is greater than what is shown. The number of icons were reduced for editorial reasons.

To begin a Chameleon PPP session, double-click the "Custom" icon. This icon

113

invokes the TCP/IP Chameleon program that dials into your provider's host, which passes your dial-up to a PPP connection to the Internet. When you open the Custom icon, Chameleon presents you with the dialog box in Figure 25-2. To start your dial-up, click on the word "Connect" on the menu bar.

Your Internet provider can help you configure Chameleon with the information it needs to dial the provider's modem and hook to a PPP or SLIP connection.

The kind of information Custom needs is basically two fold:

- IP router related info such as your PC's IP address, the FQDN of your Internet provider, and so on.

- modem dialing information such as what serial port it is on, its initialization string, baud rate, and so forth.

Configuring Custom is a bit more involved than configuring other Windows based TCP/IP applications because Custom demands information in a few more areas that the other programs. Once you've done this once, doing it again will be less of a chore and will help you understand what competing applications need in the way of configuring data.

Finally, pay attention while you're configuring Custom (and others). Learn why certain information is going into specific blocks. You will understand the process and be able to help yourself and others later.

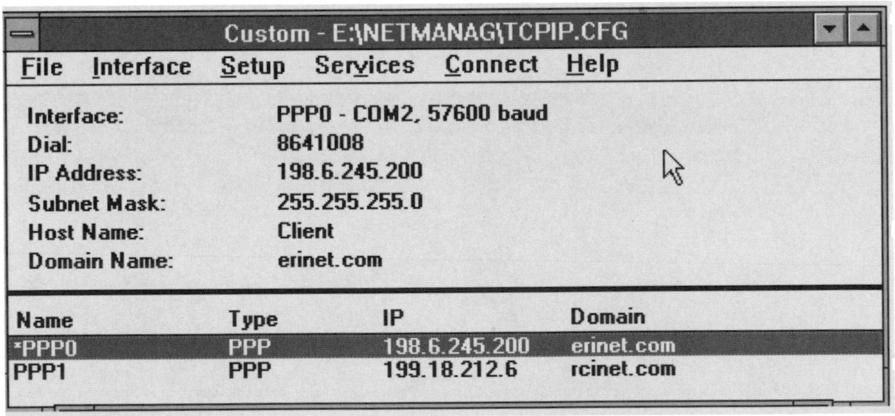

Figure 25-2

114

CHAPTER 26
CHAMELEON E-MAIL

E-MAIL WITH A PPP SESSION

For this section of the tutorial, locate the icon for the e-mail client program.

Although this lesson features Chameleon e-mail, other worthy third party Winsock compliant e-mail programs exist. One excellent application is *PCEudora* from Qualcomm. Find it at ftp address `ftp.qualcomm.com, cd /quest/windows/eudora/1.4`.

The Chameleon mail program is full-featured. Once online, double-click the "Mailbox" icon to begin an e-mail session. The dialog box in Figure 26-1 appears.

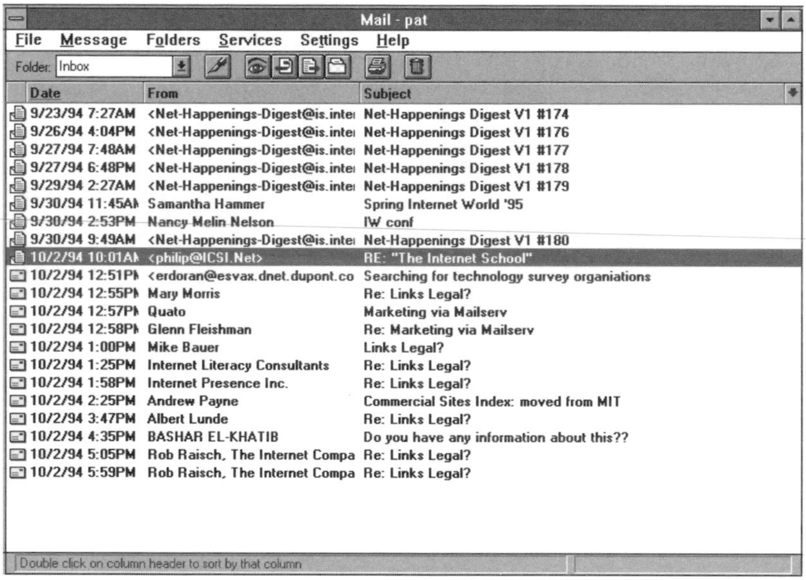

Figure 26-1

Here are some items of note in Figure 26-1:

• The "page" icon to the left of the top nine messages indicates that the user read those messages.

• The "envelope" icon to the left of the rest of the messages indicates that the user has not yet read those messages.

• The bar across the ninth message is the selected message. If you hit `<Enter>` or click on it with the mouse, the message will open for you to read.

• The "pen" icon on the icon bar creates a new message.

• The "eye" icon reads a selected message (in this case, message nine).

• The "printer" icon prints the selected message so you can keep a hard copy of it.

• The "trashcan" icon deletes the selected message. You can select multiple messages and delete them all at once.

There is a significant difference between mail management through a terminal emulation session (Pine, normally) and a PPP connection through a program such as Chameleon. When you load Pine and process your e-mail through terminal emulation, the actual physical file storing the mail message is on your provider's host server.

With PPP service, your provider uses **Post Office Protocol** to store your incoming E-mail on his mail server. When you log into an E-mail session, POP sends physical copies of your messages to your hard drive, transferring them one at a time. The upside to this is that you have all your E-mail on your hard drive and can read your E-mail after you log off your PPP session. The downside is that this transfer can take quite a while if you lots of mail. Be sure to delete unwanted messages; if you don't, your hard drive will steadily fill with old e-mail.

Figure 26-2 shows the result of clicking the "pen" icon to prepare a new E-mail message.

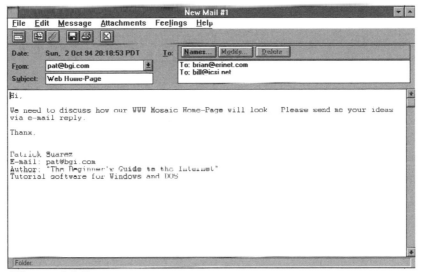

Figure 26-2

Here are the major features of Figure 26-2:

• The "arrow-overletter" icon sends your message.

• The "paper clip" icon attaches a file to the message.

• The "disk" icon saves your message to a file on your hard drive.

• The "printer" icon prints the message.

• The "X" icon cancels the message without sending it.

Note the .sig file, which Chameleon Mail automatically places into every outgoing message.

Something to keep in mind....

If you are on the road a lot, consider the pros and cons of this type of mail service, including this: If you process mail through a shell account and Pine (or Unix mailx), you can perform a simple, text based telnet session from another Internet account elsewhere to read and answer e-mail at virtually no cost to you.

If you use a PPP access, you probably will be forced to make a long distance call to enter your account, then spend time using Post Office Protocol to download perhaps dozens of messages to your laptop PC.

Now you see why your author uses a shell account and Pine to process his mail. Although a clever provider tech can shuttle PPP account mail into more easily accessible channels, the power of Pine and the ease of shell and telnet access make e-mailing a much less complicated experience!

CHAPTER 27
CHAMELEON TELNET

Chameleon Telnet creates a terminal emulation session on a window on your screen.

The procedure is a no-brainer:

• Find the Telnet icon (it has a telephone and a net...the essence of cleverness...).

• Double click on it to open it. You will see a dialog box that will ask for the telnet address of your destination (host), the port number (normally, leave this set at 23 unless you see a specific port number in a telnet address), and the emulation (use the default of VT-100, unless you know for sure that it is different, in which case you would select from the drop down list presented in this field). See Figure 27-1.

Once you have clicked on the "OK" button, your remote login session appears, as in Figure 27-2. As always, make note of the escape sequence established for the remote host to which you telneted. Keep in mind that you are in a terminal emulation telnet session while you are connected to the remote site.

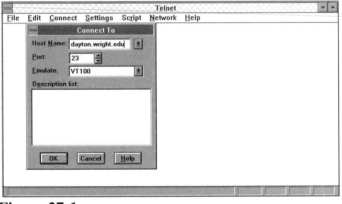

Figure 27-1

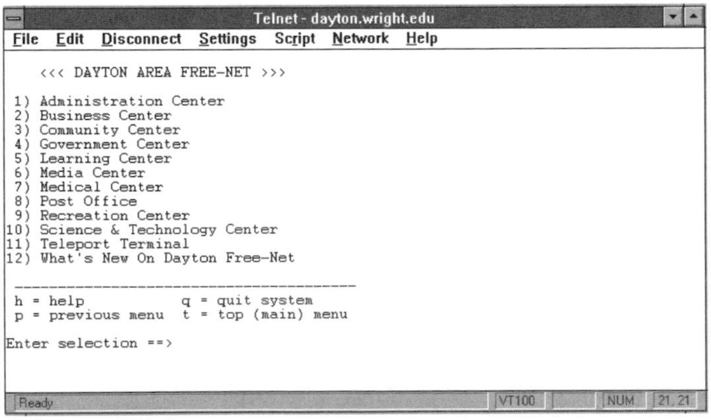

Figure 27-2

To leave your remote session, proceed through the normal logout steps at the remote site or click on the word "Disconnect" on the menu bar.

CHAPTER 28
GRAPHICAL FTP

File Transfer Protocol is a complex subject whose execution is made easy by Chameleon's ftp program. Older Chameleon ftp programs could not read certain types of ftp servers, so ensure that you have the latest version. Opening the ftp icon and logging into an ftp site will get you the screen in Figure 28-1.

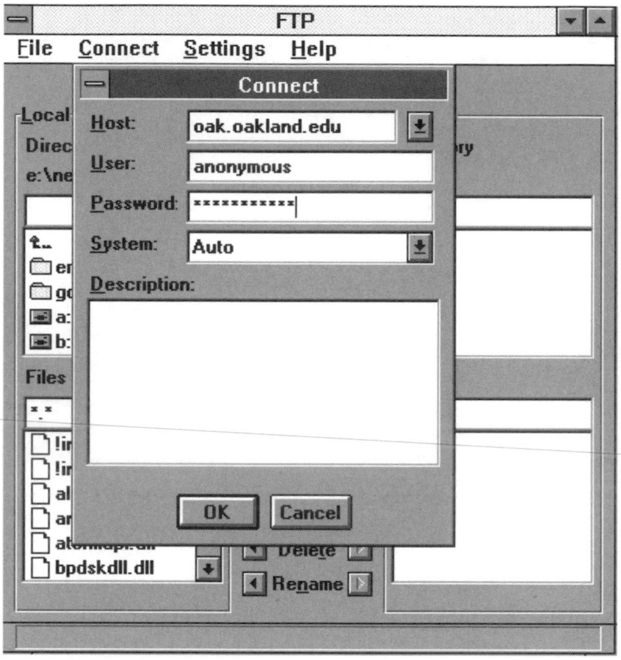

Figure 28-1

The opening dialog has fields for the ftp host address name, your "anonymous" login ID, and e-mail address password.

Figure 28-2 shows the simplified ftp interface. Notice in Figure 28-2 that the ftp dialog box is separated into three major vertical sections:

- The left third of the box maps your computer's hard drive.

- The middle third contains ftp commands, including ASCII and Binary selector buttons.

- The right third of the box maps the remote ftp host's directories and files.

When you have reached this screen, your ftp session is ready to go. You simply click on the directory names on the right third of the screen (in the upper box that displays the directory names) until you reach the directory you need. The file names contained in the directories appear in the larger white box below the directory-name box. When you find the file name you want, set the Binary type (if necessary), set the target drive and directory on your computer, and select the < Copy button in the center of the ftp box. See Figure 28-2.

122

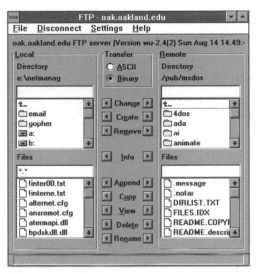

Figure 28-2

To leave your ftp session, click on the word "Disconnect" on the menu bar.

FTP through a World Wide Web session, using the Netscape browser, is simpler because it anticipates file types and display subdirectories more quickly. Notice in Figure 28-3 that the "Location" box lists the URL *ftp://ftp.erinet.com/pub/winsock;* the files residing under that subdirectory are listed in the main box below that.

We started the ftp session by entering the URL `ftp://ftp.erinet.com`. Once Netscape took us to that ftp host, we saw the subdirectories displayed in blue letters[10] on the Netscape screen. We clicked on the blue word *pub,* then on the ensuing blue word *winsock.* At this last step, we saw the listing of files that you see in Figure 28-3. To download one of those files to your hard drive, you just click on its blue name. No muss, no fuss. Mosaic can do this, too.

The terminal emulation equivalent to this URL would have been:

% `ftp ftp.erinet.com`, then <Enter>.

ftp> `cd pub/winsock`, then <Enter>.

ftp> `binary`, then <Enter> .(because the listed files from which we would choose are binary)

ftp> `get <file name>`, then <Enter>.

After all of this, you would still have to start a Zmodem download session to carry the file from your provider's host server to your PC.

---

[10]Netscape has a handy feature shared by few other Web browsers. Once you have selected a blue word on a Netscape screen, that word changes color to purple as a reminder that you have selected it at least once.

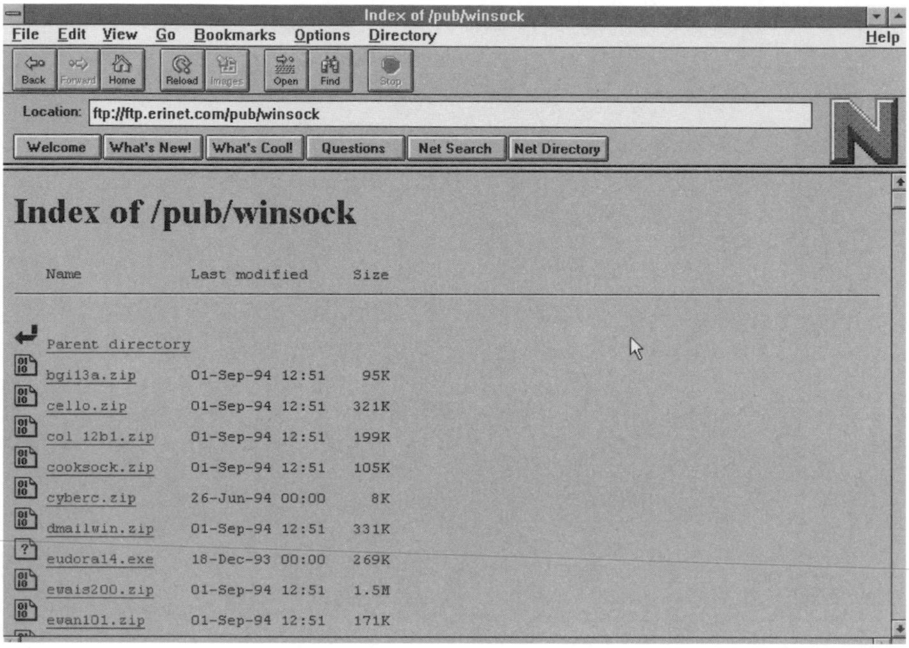

File   Edit   View   Go   Bookmarks   Options   Directory   Help

```
Back   Forward   Home      Reload  Images    Open   Find      Stop
```

Location: ftp://ftp.erinet.com/pub/winsock

```
Welcome   What's New!   What's Cool!   Questions   Net Search   Net Directory
```

Index of /pub/winsock

```
Name              Last modified       Size


  Parent directory
  bgi13a.zip      01-Sep-94 12:51     95K
  cello.zip       01-Sep-94 12:51     321K
  col_12b1.zip    01-Sep-94 12:51     199K
  cooksock.zip    01-Sep-94 12:51     105K
  cyberc.zip      26-Jun-94 00:00      8K
  dmailwin.zip    01-Sep-94 12:51     331K
  eudora14.exe    18-Dec-93 00:00     269K
  ewais200.zip    01-Sep-94 12:51     1.5M
  ewan101.zip     01-Sep-94 12:51     171K
```

Figure 28-3

There is a marvelous Winsock compliant ftp called *WinFTP*, one of the best around. Use Archie to find the file name winftp.zip. This is an outstanding piece of software, and you should look for it if you plan to do a lot of file transferring.

For those who want ftp to be as simple an operation as possible, using some sort of graphical Web browser for ftp has benefits over older methods if they intend to perform a lot of file transfers to their PCs. Don't forget: with The Internet Adapter or Slipknot, you can use Netscape through a Unix shell account.

CHAPTER 29
GRAPHICAL GOPHER

Although Chameleon presents a useful, if overly-busy, Gopher interface (see Figure 29-1), the best tool to generate a Gopher session is Netscape by way of a Gopher URL (gopher://gopher......). Nevertheless, Chameleon Gopher is a complete application which includes a bookmark feature.

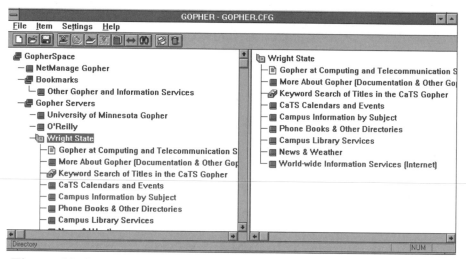

Figure 29-1

Proceeding through Gopher menu levels is as simple as clicking on a Gopher menu icon such as a file cabinet or red box. If you configure your Chameleon Gopher viewer to recognize .GIF and .JPG image files, it will display pictures, too. To close a Chameleon Gopher session, click on *File,* then *Exit* from the menu bar.

Gopher through Netscape is perhaps a quicker road to a Gopher session. Figure 29-2 shows the URL gopher://gopher.internic.net in the "Location" box and the Gopher menu items below there. Clicking on a menu item takes you to more menus.

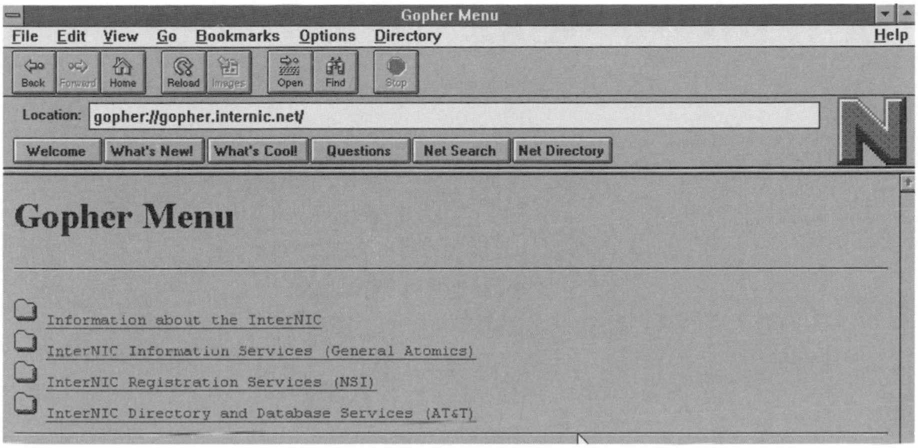

Figure 29-2

Gopher is such an easy concept and tool, it really amounts to nothing more than entering a gopher address, the using a mouse to click your way from menu to menu. It is ironic, given the overly-complex age in which we live, that something so powerful and useful is so simple to execute.

CHAPTER 30
GRAPHIC NEWSREADERS

The Chameleon newsreader that NetManage released in early 1995 fixed a flaw in the previous versions; the old version of NEWTNews displayed a maximum of 6,500 newsgroup titles. The newest edition lifts that limit.

The first time you use NEWTNews, you must configure it with your Login ID and password. Hint: It usually likes the same Login ID and password you used with Chameleon e-mail.

Once you open a news session, NEWTNews updates the newsgroups to which you previously subscribed. See Figure 30-1. The "+ folder" icon pulls in all the newsgroup names it can to allow you to subscribe to additional newsgroups. The main display area shows the names of your subscribed newgroups, how many postings within each one exist ("Total"), and how many are "unread".

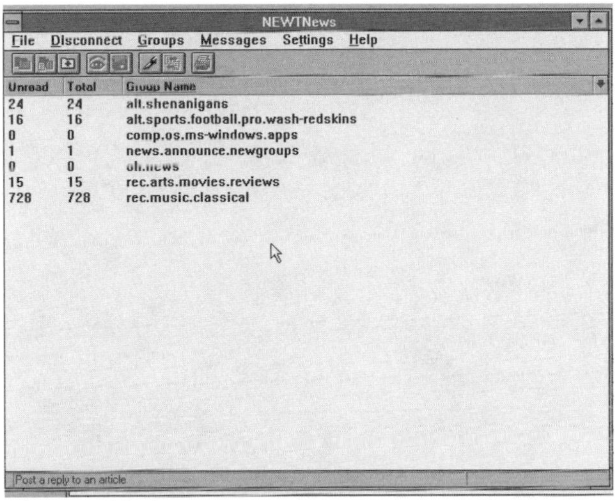

Figure 30-1

Clicking on a newsgroup name will open the group and show the available postings. Clicking a **rec.arts.movies.reviews** produced the results in Figure 30-2.

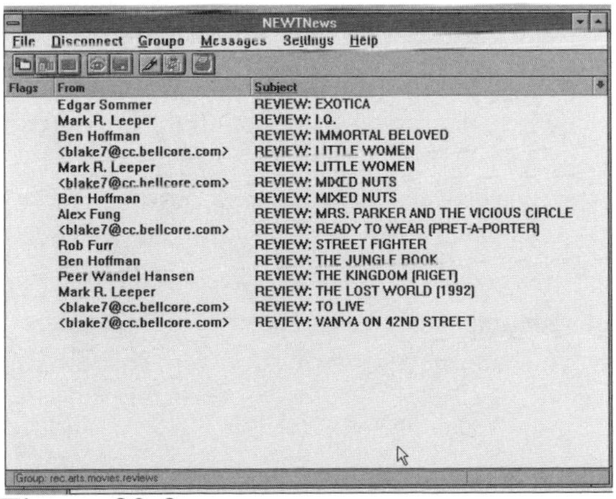

Figure 30-2

The newsreader that accompanies Netscape is full-featured. You access it by selecting the word *Directory* from the menu bar. The next step is to select *Go to Newsgroups* from the ensuing drop down menu. Later versions of Netscape may return the newsreader icon to the button bar. It was on early versions, but disappeared even though the news capability remained. See Figure 30-3.

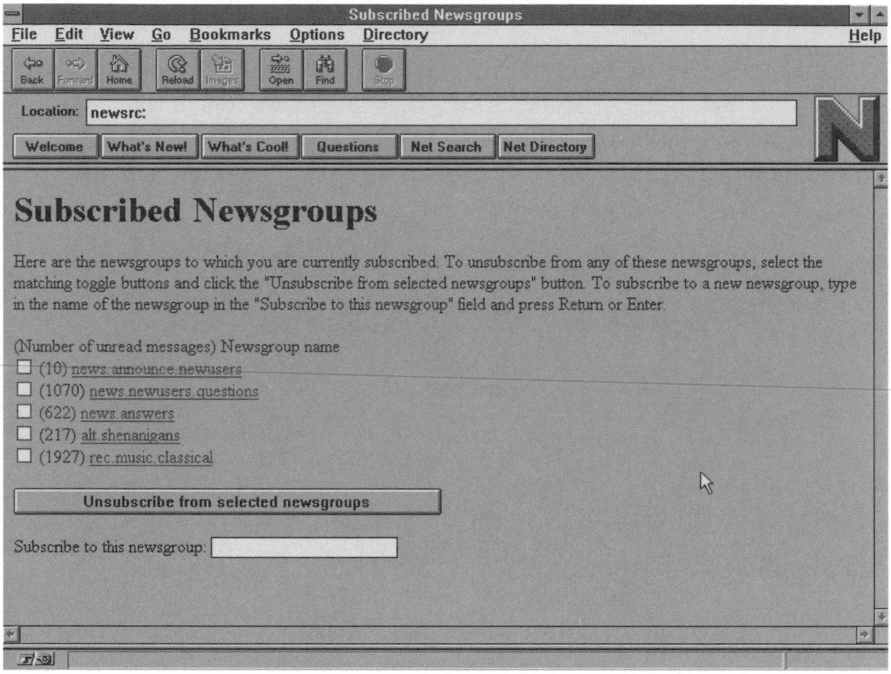

Figure 30-3

Here's how to "yank" all the available topics and postings into view:

1. In the block that lets you enter the name of a newsgroup to which you wish to subscribe, enter * . *.

2. Click the subscribe bar. Netscape will add *.* to the list of subscribed news-groups.

3. Finally, click *.* to display the names of all the newsgroups.

Using the Netscape newsreader, you can read postings, reply to them, and send new ones. Unsubscribing and subscribing to specific newsgroups are both easy tasks, too.

Clicking the **alt.shenanigans** news group produced the screen in Figure 30-4. As with all newsreaders, you can reply to postings or start new discussions with original postings.

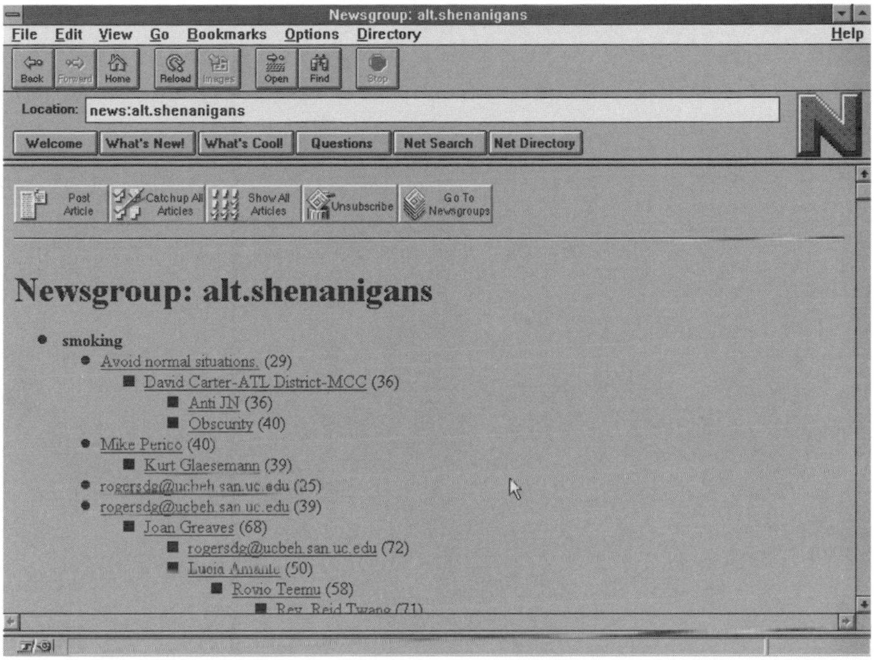

![Newsgroup: alt.shenanigans browser window]

Window title bar: Newsgroup: alt.shenanigans

Menu: File Edit View Go Bookmarks Options Directory   Help

Toolbar: Back Forward Home Reload Images Open Find Stop

Location: news:alt.shenanigans

Welcome | What's New! | What's Cool! | Questions | Net Search | Net Directory

Post Article | Catchup All Articles | Show All Articles | Unsubscribe | Go To Newsgroups

Newsgroup: alt.shenanigans

- smoking
  - Avoid normal situations. (29)
    - David Carter-ATL District-MCC (36)
      - Anti JN (36)
      - Obscurity (40)
  - Mike Perico (40)
    - Kurt Glaesemann (39)
  - rogersdg@ucbeh.san.uc.edu (25)
  - rogersdg@ucbeh.san.uc.edu (39)
    - Joan Greaves (68)
      - rogersdg@ucbeh.san.uc.edu (72)
    - Luoia Amante (50)
      - Rovio Teemu (58)
        - Rev. Reid Twane (71)

Figure 30-4

CHAPTER 31
THE GRAPHICAL WORLD WIDE WEB

Nothing related to the Internet has caused a bigger sensation than graphical World Wide Web browsers. These graphical browsers make sophisticated links to Web, telnet, ftp, WAIS, Gopher, newsgroup, and other sessions. The beauty of a Mosaic or a Netscape is that it does so seamlessly: You just click on a blue word or an image with a blue border, and the link occurs quickly and, to your eyes, easily.

Everything you can do with the Lynx browser described in Chapter 22 can be done with such programs as Netscape, Mosaic, WebSurfer, AirMosaic, Winweb, and Cello. These programs, created for such graphical environments as Windows, Mac, and X-Windows, offer color pictures, full-motion video, stereo sound, and multi-type-face text presentations of data culled from any Internet resource.

Mosaic was first, having been born in 1993 at the National Center for Supercomputing Applications at the University of Illinois, Urbana-Champaign. Mosaic for Windows is available in an older 16-bit form and newer 32-bit form. You can get both from ftp site `ftp.ncsa.uiuc.edu`. If you download the 32-bit version, you must also download and install the 32-bit Windows drivers if your system does not already have them. After download and installation, you must configure Mosaic to your system and your Internet provider's system. If you are not up to this task, your Internet provider can help.

Cello and **Winweb** followed, then **AirMosaic** and **WebSurfer**, and are worthy programs. However, this author prefers the commercial Web browser, **Netscape.**

Netscape and Mosaic offers several improvements to Mosaic, among them:

• Faster loading of images and text to the screen.

• Image memory. When you load a URL, Netscape and Mosaic file the URL's images away. Then, when you revisit that same URL, the images that have not changed appear on the screen almost immediately, loading from a hard drive cache, not from the URL site.

• As mentioned previously, if you click on a blue hypertext word in Netscape, it turns purple as a signal that you have already opened that text link. The same holds true for images which are surrounded by blue borders. With Mosaic, the blue characters turn red.

Netscape is significant because of these features:

• Compatibility with some URLs. Some URL hosts code their http documents to work better with Netscape than with other browsers. They even warn you if you access them with something other than Netscape.

• Netscape has its own file viewer for opening .BMP, .GIF, and .JPG image files.

• Netscape knows when a file is trying to load to the hard drive, and issues a confirming question at the beginning of the download procedure.

Netscape is available from `ftp.mcom.com` or its mirror sites. It, too, needs installation and configuration, and, perhaps, assistance from your Net provider.

Netscape and Mosaic require a mouse, at least 8MB of system RAM, fast video, and some assistant files which are available from ftp sites. Here are the files that both need.

Netscape needs:

• MPEGPLAY to play back video.

• MPLAYER or WHAM to play back sound.

• WIN32 for the latest 32-bit version.

Mosaic needs:

• LVIEW to view .BMP, .GIF, and .JPG images.

• MPEGPLAY to play back video.

• MPLAYER or WHAM to play back sound.

• WIN32 for the latest 32-bit version.

With the advent of programs such as *The Internet Adapter* and *Slipknot*, Netscape and Mosaic are available to users with common Unix shell accounts, as well as to those with traditional PPP and SLIP accounts and direct, dedicated feed access. See Chapter 22 for information about TIA and Slipknot.

To launch **Mosaic,** click on its icon. It is in the bottom row of icons in Figure 25-1, Chapter 25. When you load a URL, the Mosaic globe in the screen's upper right hand corner will spin. While entertaining, the spinning globe is not what should have your attention. You should watch the thin bottom panel on the screen, where you will see the status of the URL's loading procedure. You can choose to have any URL, or no URL, automatically load when you start a Mosaic Web session.

See Figure 31-1, the 32-bit Mosaic interface. In it, note the following:

• On the row of icon buttons, there are six to which you should pay special attention:

♦ The "disk" icon: Saves incoming data, including data from ftp files.

♦ The "+ flaming page" icon: Saves a URL to your "hot list", to which you can refer to recall URLs you like. This feature is similar to Gopher's bookmark.

♦ The "printer" icon: Lets you print the contents of the current page.

♦ The left right arrow icon: You can return to the previous link by clicking here.

◆   The "rolled newspaper" icon is a newsreader.

◆   The "envelope in slot" icon is an e-mail client program that sends messages.

• The long white rectangular box below the icon buttons is where you enter your URL. The URL that is listed in Figure 31-1 is NCSA's Weather World where you can see the latest weather images via satellite.

• The picture image to the left of the words, "U.S. Surface Weather Map". The picture is surrounded by a blue border, which means you can click on it for a bigger image.

• The blue words below the satellite image. They are blue, which means that you link to (in this case) satellite photos if you click on them.

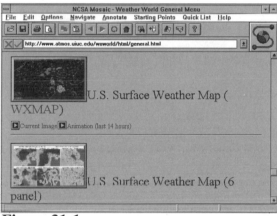

Figure 31-1

When you add a URL to your "hot list", Mosaic adds it to the *Starting Points* list, available as the sixth item on the menu bar. See Figure 31-2.

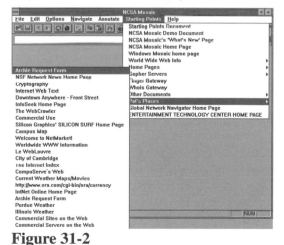

Figure 31-2

135

To launch **Netscape,** click its icon. Again, see Figure 25-1. Netscape's interface is somewhat simpler than Mosaic's. See Figure 31-3.

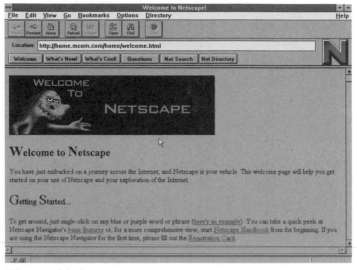

Figure 31-3

Two icons from the icon button bar to note are "Open" and "Find". The former presents a window into which you type the URL you wish to visit; the latter allows you search through the text on the current URL that's on-screen. To set a bookmark, click on the word *Boomarks,* then *Add Bookmark*, on the menu bar. As with Mosaic, you can monitor incoming activity at the lower left corner of the Netscape screen.

An increasingly common mistake is to consider a graphical browser such as Netscape or Mosaic as interchangeable with the Internet tool World Wide Web. Remember: The World Wide Web is a hypertext-based Internet resource that links thousands of hosts; Netscape and Mosaic are two graphical browser that present the Web to you. Do not get into the habit of referring to the World Wide Web as Mosaic or Netscape, as in "a Mosaic site".

Ease of use and flexible features make the Internet a smooth and enjoyable experience with Mosaic and, especially, Netscape. With the advent of *The Internet Adapter* and *Slipknot* and the fairly simple installation of (especially) Netscape, nearly everyone can surf the Net with style.

And the latest entry into the Web browser sweepstakes...

NetManage's WebSurfer is the Net's newest browser. It features a caching system, as does Netscape and a familiar interface based on Mosaic and Netscape. WebSurfer also allows technically skilled folks to enter Web files and tinker with their structure. Future versions of the Chameleon suite package will include WebSurfer.

PART 4
The Internet in Business

INTERNET BUSINESS STRATEGIES AND TACTICS

What was a strictly non-commercial, academic medium is now a powerful instrument of commerce. With the explosion of Internet popularity has come full-scale entrepreneurial activity, some of it welcome, some of it controversial. Organizations that previously never gave a second thought to computers, bulletin board systems, networks, and those who populate them suddenly became entranced with the vision of using the Internet to advertise everything under the sun to a group of people considered to be upscale, educated, sophisticated, and moneyed. These marketers saw low advertising costs (sending thousands or millions of e-mail messages costs virtually nothing compared with printing brochures and letters, buying address lists, putting everything together, and paying postage) and the immediacy of electronic messaging (compared with the days land-based mail takes). They made some classic mistakes, among them misjudging and underestimating an audience because they did not bother to get to know the on-line culture.

But, the Internet is an excellent way to sell goods and services, if a company knows how to do it.

Here are some steps that could lead to marketing success:

- Get connected with at least a PPP or SLIP account. A full-time, dedicated, 56K line is preferable.

- Don't do anything anywhere until you are fully familiar with what the culture will tolerate.

- Create strategies that support your company's goals, and tactics that support those strategies. Internet marketing must be just one tactic/strategy within an overall goal-oriented marketing plan. It will need support from other, related media (magazines, newsletters, etc.) to succeed.

- Know that marketing is more than just advertising. Create a campaign within the guidelines of online advertising. Include print ads in selected publications that tie back to online initiatives.

- Never, ever hit electronic mail addresses, mailing lists, and newsgroups with unsolicited, cold-call ads. This is the surest way to electronic disaster. The retribution from online citizens will be swift and creative. They might send hundreds of megabytes of junk to your e-mail address, putting it out of commission for a long time. They might lobby your ISP to discontinue your connection. Don't do it, ever. Just because you have the tool does not mean that you automatically know how to use it. Get online and probe all Internet resources as thoroughly as possible before developing a strategy based on it.

- If you want to take, you have to give. Establish gopher and World Wide Web sites. Invite people in to sample your goods. Give something away, be it product, advice, or information. This creates good will and makes people want to

138

return to your electronic site to do business with you. Don't be afraid to use subtle marketing techniques in your gopher and Web space.

- Create an e-mail address for free customer support. Answer your mail quickly, thoroughly, and courteously.

- Create an effective .sig file that gracefully promotes your company or product.

- Establish automatic e-mail response. Programs that automatically respond to special incoming addresses (e.g., info@product.com) enable your company to have an immediate and inexpensive method of transmitting marketing data.

- Get your own Internet domain name, then put it on every print media you can, especially business cards.

- As appropriate, create a file transfer protocol site and archive information there for people to download, for free.

- Consider your competition and your customer base. What technology do they know and use? Are you ahead of them or behind them?

- Stay current in your industry by monitoring (and sometimes contributing to) appropriate newsgroups and mailing lists. You might even begin to subtly influence your industry by doing this.

- Hire people who are deeply familiar with the plumbing of the Internet and who can manage your site. Or, pay "rent" on another Internet site that sells space (especially World Wide Web space) until you can afford your own. Sometimes renting is smarter than purchasing.

- Create a colorful, effective World Wide Web home page that is informative and packs a multimedia wallop.

- Convince as many influential World Wide Web sites as possible to establish pointers within their home pages to your home page. The more links you have throughout the system, the more people will visit your Web site.

- Don't expect miracles. There might be several million people with Internet access, but they will not beat a path to your doorstep without a lot of effort on your part.

- Eliminate hype! Don't market on the Internet as if it were television. On TV, flash and volume sell products; not so on the Net.

SECURITY

Security is a major concern on something as free-wheeling and wide-open as the Internet. If you've got hardware and software resources to protect, construct a firewall. As shown in Figure 5-4, in Chapter 5, a firewall is a free-standing computer that filters all traffic trying to enter a host system.

If you want your correspondence to be private, use encryption software such as *Pretty Good Privacy*, described in the next section. Always use antivirus software on your system even though your ISP probably uses it. Finally, always create an effective password and never give it to anyone.

ENCRYPTION

The Internet is a public place, and access to the bits that flow from router to router is free and easy. To protect sensitive data from prying eyes, a system of **encryption keys** exists. A *key* is a string of alphabetic, numeric, and special characters that is needed to unscramble (decode) encrypted messages.

With **private key encryption**, one person gives the decoding key information to another person. There is a significant amount of trust with private key encryption because either party could compromise the key.

The most popular encryption program is called *Pretty Good Privacy*. Once you get to know its intricacies, it's reasonably easy to use.

Because of some hassles the U.S. Government gave to PGP's author, you'll have to work just a bit to download it. First, telnet to the site net—dist.mit.edu, then log in as getpgp. you will have to answer four questions related to your citizenship. Once through that drill, the site will direct you to the PGP file.

Public key encryption is more secure because two keys are involved. With public key encryption, you publish your *public* key. A person wishing to send you an encrypted message will encode his outbound message using your public key. When the encoded message arrives, you decode it with the other key called the *private* key, which only you have.

Key escrow is a controversial government program that gives federal law enforcement officials the right to access your encrypted messages. The decoding key is broken into multiple parts, with several individuals or agencies each holding parts of the key. Only by consensus by all key-holders can access be granted to your data.

The federal government's **Clipper chip** program is a hardware-based technology that offers decryption capabilities to fax machines, modems, computers, and other communication devices. Clipper technology enables access to communications without the knowledge of the targeted person. Because of the potential for abuse by any law enforcement agency that possesses the know-how, many public and private agencies have lobbied hard against the adoption of Clipper technology in communication hardware.

KEEPING UP WITH CHANGES

First, subscribe to the *net-happenings* mailing list. <u>Nothing</u> keeps you better informed about daily Internet changes than Gleason Sackman's labor of love. To subscribe, use this e-mail address: `majordomo@is.internic.net`. In the text body, enter just these words: `subscribe net-happenings-digest`. You will receive net-happenings in "digest" form–many announcements in just a few (lengthy) e-mail messages.

Second, subscribe to newsletter, Jayne Levin's *Internet Letter*. Reach Levin at 800-NET-WEEK.

Third, subscribe to *Internet World, Online Access*, and *Boardwatch* magazines.

A BIT OF HISTORY...

Here is a brief look at key events and years in the history of the Net.

1957: The Soviet Union launches Sputnik. One U.S. response is to form the Advanced Research Projects Agency (ARPA) whose mission is to develop ways to put U.S. technology ahead of foreign powers and keep it there. ARPA later becomes DARPA, with the D standing for Defense.

1962: Packet-switching technology is proposed. The goal is for one computer to "talk" to any other computer regardless of its type.

1969: The first network designed with the vision of 1962 in mind. The protocol behind this success is the NCP, Network Control Protocol.

1972: E-mail is born.

1973: The fledgling packet-switching network goes international to Great Britain and Norway.

1979: USENET newsgroups are born.

1981: The concept of mailing lists is born with the BITNET.

1982: TCP/IP replaces NCP as the primary "interneting" protocol.

1984: The FQDN system is born.

1986: NSFNet, the non-profit National Science Foundation Network, is born. NSFNet links educational institutions, the government, the military, think tanks, and the five supercomputing centers.

1989: The World Wide Web is born.

1990: The original ARPANet is retired.

1991: Gopher and WAIS are born. CIX, the Commercial Internet Exchange, is also born to give some weight to commercial companies who want to "Internet" and send packets around the commercially-owned backbones. These backbones have links to the NSFNet, so that the aforementioned noncommercial facilities have communication access to the commercial backbones.

1993: Mosaic is born.

1994: The NSFNet is shut down, to be converted to the VBNS, the Very High Speed Backbone Network Service that will interlink the five supercomputing centers. The Internet becomes a commercial entity, with all backbones owned by telecommunications and Internet companies. CIX encounters major difficulties as many members abandon ship. Netscape is born.

1995: The 'Big Five" online services add comprehensive Internet access changing the landscape of the Net permanently.

GLOSSARY AND ADDITIONAL FAQs

56k line: A medium–speed transmission line that moves data at the rate of 57,600 bits per second.

Anonymous ftp: The ability to log into an ftp host system without having an account at that system.

ARPAnet: A Government sponsored packet–switching network that, ultimately, grew into the Internet as it is today.

Archie: A program that maintains a catalog of the contents of 1,300 FTP host systems. Archie is client software or accessed through telnet or Gopher.

Backbone: A high-speed, fiber–optic or copper–wire transmission line.

BITNET: The original set of computers that created the mailing list system. See Mailing list.

Bookmark: A placemaker in Gopher and the World Wide Web which allows a user to access an exact host address quickly.

Cello: A graphic browser for the World Wide Web that presents hypertext keywords, pictures, sound, and video.

Client: Software or hardware that accepts information from a server.

Client software: Free-standing software stored on a host that users can access and run from their computers. Client applications may also be stored on a user's own computer.

CSLIP: Compressed Serial Line Internet Protocol. Direct access to the Internet backbone by way of a modem and a dial–up account with an Internet provider.

Dedicated line: A private telephone line connecting two Internet hosts (usually a provider and a customer) that is usually medium to high–speed.

Domain type: Descriptions of Internet hosts. There are six principal domain types: com (commercial), gov (government), mil (military), edu (school), org (misc. [sometimes non–profit] organization), net (Internet provider). Countries use two–letter domains: au (Australia), uk (United Kingdom), etc.

E-mail: Electronic mail. Messages that pass from computer to computer.

E-mail format: user@host.location.domain. Example: pat@monet.icsi.net. Pat is the user; monet is the name of host computer; icsi is the location/provider; net is the domain type. Sometimes, the host name is omitted. Example: pat@bgi.com.

FAQ: Frequently Asked Question. A list of basic information, mostly for those new to the Internet, meant to help and guide (and, hopefully, diminish repetitive questions).

Flame: A vitriolic, personal attack seen most often in newsgroup postings and mailing list messages. Counterattacks on the same subject are called 'flame wars'.

FQDN: Fully Qualified Domain Name. A human–friendly equivalent to the IP address. The domain name 'bgi.com' equates to the IP address 198.6.245.121.

Freenet: A subsidized pseudo–BBS that offers a community Internet access at no charge to the community members.

FTP: File Transfer Protocol. A protocol for computer hosts that store, accept, and dispense computer files. FTP is also client software for Unix and graphical (e.g., Windows) environments.

Gateway: Access either out to other computers from within a network or access into a network from computers outside the network. Gateways can translate the messages from outside the network for the network to understand them.

Gopher: A protocol that stores information on a host for access from other systems and has a menu for a screen interface. The menus can point to other Internet tools (FTP, E-mail, Telnet, WAIS, etc). Gopher can be client software or accessed from Telnet and the World Wide Web.

Home Page: The opening screen of a World Wide Web site.

Host: A computer that dispenses information or data.

http: Hypertext Transfer Protocol. The protocol that transmits World Wide Web data.

Hypertext: A system that offers information through the use of linking keywords or pictures on a computer screen. When the highlighted word or picture is chosen, a link occurs and a new screen with different words and pictures appears, itself displaying more linked words and pictures.

Internet: A collection of nearly four million host computers that communicate using TCP/IP protocol software.

Internet access: In a terminal emulation session, a computer can have access to Internet tools and services by dialing up to another computer that is running TCP/IP software. This 'dial–up' computer is not 'on' the Internet, but accesses the Internet services of the computer to which it dials. It also uses the client software (e.g., Gopher) of the host into which it dials. VT-100 terminal emulation is usually required. See 'On the Internet'.

ISDN: Integrated Services Digital Network. A digital transmission medium for several services, among them the Internet.

IP: Internet Protocol.

IP address: A four–digit, numeric address format separated by three periods, called 'dots'. Each segment of the IP address ranges from 0 to 255. Internet routers use IP addressing to locate a destination computer. An example of an IP address is 198.6.245.121. IP addresses have FQDN equivalents. See FQDN.

IRC: Internet Relay Chat. A live, real–time tool that allows users to join discussion groups and communicate by typing words that others can see.

Knowbot: A search tool that roams through databases of white pages directories to locate people and their Internet e–mail addresses.

Leased line: See Dedicated line.

Lurk: Observing the postings of messages to newsgroups and mailing lists without sending postings of your own.

Mailing list: A subscription–based messaging system that permits many people to see a message from a user by broadcasting that message via e–mail to all who subscribe to the discussion group.

Mirror Site: an ftp host that is a clone of another ftp host.

Mosaic: A graphic browser for the World Wide Web that presents hypertext key-words, pictures, sound, and video.

MUD: Multi–User Dungeon. Interactive game–playing over telnet hosts.

Netscape: A graphic browser for the World Wide Web that presents hypertext key-words, pictures, sound, and video.

Network: A system of interconnected computers, generally with one computer, the server, as the focal point. Networks share hardware and information and allow communication from computer to computer within the system. Gateways permit communication to and from outside the network.

Newsgroup: A message–forwarding system that allows the posting and display of messages based on specific topics and areas of interest. Newsgroups are hierarchical (alt→ alt.fan→ alt.fan.dave_berry). Each level below the single word top level can contain messages. You must use a newsreader to access the postings.

Newsreader: A software tool for reading postings in newsgroups. Examples of news-readers are tin, nn, rn, and trn. There are also Windows–based client newsreaders (e.g., NetManage Chameleon Telnet) for those with PPP/SLIP/CSLIP access.

On the Internet: If your computer runs TCP/IP software, it has direct access to the Internet backbone and, therefore, to the other four million computers thus connected. This computer, with its direct backbone and router access, is 'on' the Internet. See Internet access.

Packet–switching: The Internet sends data using packet–switching. Outgoing data is chopped into packets, placed into 'electronic envelopes', and sent through a maze of routers and backbones. The packets are reassembled at the destination computer.

Ping: An application that sends a signal to an Internet host to see if it is active and the return message from that host is accurate.

POP (e–mail): Post Office Protocol. The e–mail protocol Internet providers use to distribute e–mail to customers.

POP (phone number): Point of Presence. A phone number to which a modem can dial to create an Internet session.

Port: When used with Telnet, a port number points to a specific program on a host system. Example: madlab.sprl.umich.edu 3000. The port number 3000 points to the weather program on the Michigan server.

PPP: Point–to–Point protocol. Direct access to the Internet backbone by way of a modem and a dial–up account with an Internet provider.

Protocol: A standard common to an industry.

Remote login: See Telnet.

RFC: Request for Comment. Documents that set forth the protocols and standards on which Internet technology is based.

Router: A computer that reads IP addresses and passes data packets to destination computers or other routers.

Server: A computer or software application that provides information to a client. See client.

sig: Prepared text that appears with a person's signature block in e–mail and news-group postings. Sigs can contain a person's name, phone, postal address, e–mail address, a saying, and collections of ASCII characters that create a drawing.

SLIP: Serial Line Internet Protocol. Direct access to the Internet backbone by way of a modem and a dial–up account with an Internet provider

T1 line: A high–speed (1.54 megabits per second) Internet transmission line.

T3 line: A high–speed (45 megabits per second) Internet transmission line.

TCP/IP: The software that contains the protocols that enable computers of dissimilar types communicate with each other over copper phone lines, fiber optic cable, and satellites. TCP (Transmission Control Protocol) chops outgoing data into packets and reassembles the packets. IP (Internet Protocol) routes the packets.

Telnet: A protocol to log into networks outside of your network or computer as if you were logging in there at that remote site. Also called remote login. Telnet can be client software in the Unix or graphical (e.g., Windows) environments.

Terminal emulation: A protocol in which a computer 'becomes' a temporary VT–100 terminal connected to a host server. See VT–100.

Unix shell: A screen interface to the Unix operating system and the services it pro-vides. The prompt is usually a %, $,or > symbol. Think of a Unix shell as being similar to the standard DOS interface that presents a C: prompt. From the prompt, you can issue commands to run software programs, etc.

URL: Universal Resource Locator. A protocol that finds host sites in FTP, Gopher, and World Wide Web systems.

USENET: The original set of computers that created the newsgroup system. See Newsgroup.

Veronica: A search tool that reads Gopher menu titles and helps you find information on Gopher servers.

VT–100: Terminal emulation protocol needed for computers dialing into an Internet provider's host system. Thus connected, the computer that dialed up becomes a terminal on the host system. The VT–100 emulation provides a screen cursor. VT–320 emulation can also be used.

WAIS: Wide Area Information Server. About 500 hosts that store information on a variety of subjects. Users can find information by issuing keywords that search through the content of the documents on the WAIS machines.

WebSurfer: A graphic browser for the World Wide Web that presents hypertext keywords, pictures, sound, and video.

Winsock: Windows Socket. Software that sits between client applications and the TCP/IP program and allows those applications to make calls to TCP/IP.

WinWeb: A graphic browser for the World Wide Web that presents hypertext keywords, pictures, sound,and video.

World Wide Web: A system of host computers that stores and presents information in a succession of hypertext screens. The Web employs other Internet tools (FTP, Gopher, E–mail, WAIS, Telnet) from its page of hypertext words and pictures.

Additional FAQs

Q. I got an "out-of-memory" error when running Windows based terminal emulation or TCP/IP software. What do I do?
A. Make sure that you are in 386 Enhanced Mode and that you have a sufficiently large, permanent swap file. If you do not understand these concepts, see your Windows manual. Also, make sure that you have no other programs, such as screen savers, running. Other factors, such as the number of icons and number of program groups in Windows' Program Manager, the number of colors instructed to display (you only need 256), and the screen resolution (you need no more than 800X600, and 640X480 is adequate for most users) all affect your available memory.

Q. When I try to connect, I get login ID or password invalid errors. What do I do?
A. Your login ID and password are case sensitive. That is, if you established your ID and password in all lower case, you must type all lower case letters or numbers. Beyond that, ask for help from your Internet provider.

Q. Can I change my login ID?
A. Yes, but you will have to do this with the help of your Internet provider. Be careful when creating your login ID because it is someone else's first impression of you.

Q. How do I change my password?
A. Consult with your Internet provider, and do it in cooperation with him or her because you do not want to confuse your provider's terminal or host server. Many network experts feel that changing a password frequently is a wise practice.

Q. Where should I send comments about my Internet provider's service?
A. Many Internet providers create their own set of local newsgroups, such as "<provider>.news.announcements". These are not normally distributed to other news servers throughout the news system.

Q. How do I cancel my Internet account?
A. You must give written notice, although many providers allow internal e-mail messages to sign off for good. Read your contract's fine print to ensure that you get a refund for the unused portion of any prepaid long–term arrangement.

Q. Why should I turn off call waiting on my phone service? How do I do it?
A. When call waiting detects an incoming call, it sends a signal to your phone number. This signal will disconnect a modem while it is online. To temporarily disable call waiting, place the following character string at the front of the number string your modem must dial to reach a provider: *70, Don't forget the comma (which creates a one-second delay to allow the call waiting to kick in). As soon as your session concludes and the modem hangs up, call waiting is automatically brought back to life.

Q. Can I use my shell account login ID and password with my PPP account, if I have both?
A. Only if you prearrange this with your Internet provider. He or she can make them the same.

Q. Can I read e-mail offline?

A. If you have a PPP or SLIP account and use a graphical Winsock compliant e-mail reader such as Eudora, you will download incoming e-mail as files to your hard drive. After you sign off your session, you can then read the messages offline. If you have a shell account, the e-mail files are located on your provider's mail server and you normally read them while they are there. You may, however, save each message as a file, then transfer the files to your hard drive, and read each file with an ASCII text editor.

Q. Can I use third party shareware with my PPP account?

A. Yes, if it is Winsock compliant. Most TCP/IP shareware is Winsock compliant. See "Winsock compliant" elsewhere in this tutorial.

Q. How do I subscribe to a newsgroup that's not listed?

A. Use your newsreader to call it up, then take whatever steps are necessary (hitting the letter S in tin, for example) to "subscribe" (add the newsgroup to your list of news files automatically listed for access by your newsreader). If your provider's news server does not carry that particular newsgroup, you're out of luck.

Q. How do I use picture files posted to newsgroups? They look like ASCII text!

A. Newsreaders such as tin exist in an ASCII text world where binary image files are strangers. Users that want to share image files must use a process called "uuencoding", in which they use a program called UUENCODE. UUENCODE temporarily translates the binary file to an ASCII file that, to an ASCII text reader such as VEDIT, looks like incomprehensible trash. A corresponding program called UUDECODE reformulates the temporary ASCII file back to its original binary state. Suppose you had a file called MYDOG.PCX that you wished to share with the world. You would process MYDOG.PCX with UUENCODE, and a new file called MYDOG.UUE would be created. You would post MYDOG.UUE to a newsgroup, where some pet lover would download it, process it with UUDECODE, and then have another file called MYDOG.PCX. Some newsreaders can automatically process uuencoded files for you. Also, some binary images are so large, that UUENCODE breaks them into a series of files (1 of x, 2 of x, 3 of x, and so on). Programs exist that will put all the files together in order, then uudecode them.

Q. How do I start a newsgroup?

A. Look for the articles entitled "How to Create a New Usenet Newsgroup" and "Usenet Newsgroup Creation Companion" which appear every once in a while in the news.answers newsgroup. They are also available from the anonymous ftp site rtfm.mit.edu. Keep in mind that creating new newsgroups within the old "core" news areas such as COMP, SOC, and SCI requires a public voting process. And, once created, it's yours to administer (plan to devote lots of time to it!). Creating new newsgroups within ALT requires no voting. Therefore, nearly everything imaginable (and unimaginable) exists there...which is why ALT is so interesting!

Q. How do I turn off graphics in a WWW browser? Why would I want to?

A. Click on the word OPTIONS on the menu bar, and follow the prompts. If you're in a hurry just to get information or data, and don't need or want to download lots of pretty graphics that add nothing to the process at hand, disabling graphics will greatly speed up your data retrieval.

Q. The cache that stores my WWW browser is getting swollen with several megabytes of files. Can I get rid of them? Should I get rid of them?
A. Yes and yes. Caching is convenient because you don't have to drag lots of graphics across the Net to your hard drive once you've captured the graphics once and they haven't changed. But... But, these cache image records pile up, and most users are shocked to find that five to ten megabytes of cached information are taking up precious disk space. If you have a 28.8K modem or a faster link, empty the cache and save yourself the disk space. Besides, many people end up with a cached image for a site which they have no intention of visiting ever again.

Q. Can I print WWW pages?
A. Yes, indeed. If you have a color printer, you'll get the Web page of your choice in living color, text and images!

Q. Can I establish my own anonymous ftp subdirectory if I have a shell account?
A. Shell account users get a megabyte or so of free disk space as part of their account. Some shell account providers even allow the creation of individualized subdirectories where anonymous ftp'ers from around the world may visit. Before doing this, though, ensure that you won't get charged a ton by your provider for the privilege.

Q. The system keeps timing out when I try to access a WWW or telnet site. What's happening?
A. The site is down, temporarily or permanently, or is being hit all at once by too many users. Come back to it later. If you keep trying night and day, and the site still doesn't respond, it probably went out of business.

APPENDIX B
KEY COMMANDS

Note: Many of the commands throughout Appendix B are case-sensitive!

Major Pine Mail Reader Commands

? Help

C Compose a new message

I. Folder Index screen

L Folder List screen

A Address Book screen

S Setup functions

Q Quit Pine

Pine Compose Commands

^ Mark for deletion (usually followed by an arrow key to highlights
   text to be deleted)

^D Delete character

^X Send message   ^C Cancel message

^E Move cursor to end of line   ^A Move cursor to beginning of line

^Y Move cursor to previous page ^V Move cursor to next page

^H Backspace delete

^K Delete current line   ^U Undelete killed line

^W Search for character string   ^T Spell checker

^R Read in the contents of another file

Pine Folder Commands

A Add a new folder   G Go to another folder

Pine Read Commands

R Reply   F Forward

S Save   D Delete

P Print

Note: This list is by no means comprehensive. Pine lists all active menu items at the bottom of each screen. Consult these as required.

Major Unix Mail Reader Commands

d <message number>	Delete message
e <message number>	Edit message
m <user>	Mail message
n	Go to next message
p <message number>	Print message
q	Quit mail
r	Reply (sender only)*
R	Reply (all addresses)*
s <message> <filename>	Append message to file

* May be reversed on some systems

Major Unix Mail Creation Commands

~c <user>	Add user to carbon copy list
~e	Edit message
~m <message>	Read message text into reply
~r <file name>	Reads the contents of a file into the message
~w <file name>	Writes message into a file
~?	Prints current message

Note: ~ must be in column one (left-most column) on page.

Major Mailing List Commands

unsubscribe <list name>   Removes your name from the mailing list

signoff <list name>   Removes your name from the mailing list

review <list name>   Lists addresses of mailing list subscribers

set <list name> conceal   Keeps your address from appearing in the review command above. It does not keep your address from appearing in the From: field of the header in your submissions!

set <list name> nomail   Suspends mail delivery

set <list name> mail   Resumes mail delivery

Note: These commands get sent to the administrative mailing list address, which usually begins with: *listserv@<address>, majordomo@<address>, listproc@<address>*.

Major nn Newsreader Commands

a-z (lower case)	Select posting
N	Move to the next newsgroup
P	Move to the previous newsgroup
G	Go to a specific newsgroup
<	Moves back one menu page
>	Moves forward one menu page
K	Kills selected postings
S	Save posting to a file
R	Reply to a posting
:post	Create a new posting
M	E-mail a posting
Q	Quit nn

Major tin Newsreader Commands

/	Search for newsgroup name or header keyword.
^K	Kill selected postings
j	Go one line down
k	Go one line up
m	E-mail a posting
o	Print posting
s	Save posting to file
w	Create a new posting

Major ftp (File Transfer Protocol) Commands

ascii	Sets file type to ASCII
binary	Sets file type to binary
cd	Change directory
ls -al <or> dir	Display contents of the current subdirectory
get	Transfer a file from a remote host
mget	Transfer multiple files from a remote host
put	Transfer a file to a remote host
mput	Transfer multiple files to a remote host
pwd	Print the contents of the current subdirectory
quit	Leave ftp

Major telnet Commands

Note: The following commands are used in *command mode*.

open	Connect to a remote host
close	Disconnect from a remote host
set echo	If typed characters do not appear on screen or appear twice each on screen, use this command.
quit	Exit telnet session

ADDRESSING E-MAIL TO COMMERCIAL SYSTEMS FROM INTERNET HOSTS

Addressing E-Mail to Commercial Systems

Name of Service	How to Send...
America Online	user_name@aol.com
AT&T Mail	user_ID@attmail.com
CompuServe	nnnnn.nnnn@compuserve.com
	Note: n = a number (71410,3250).
	Note: The comma in CompuServe addressing changes to a period for Internet addressing.
Delphi	user_ID@delphi.com
Genie	user_ID@genie.geis.com
MCI Mail	nnnnnnn@mcimail.com
	Note: n = A number (1234567)
Prodigy	llllnnl@prodigy.com
	Note: l = a letter; n = a number (bjsn42a).

FIDONET

Addressing E-Mail to FIDONET requires a little explanation. FIDONET is an echomail network of more than 25,000 sites worldwide. The FIDONET is divided into six "zones". The addressing follows this pattern: n:nn/nnn. For example, the CS/2 BBS in Springfield, Ohio, has a FIDONET address of 1:110/535. So, sending Internet mail to the author of this tutorial at CS/O would take this form:

user@f535.n110.z1

Sometimes FIDONET addresses add an extra number at the end of the address: n:nn/nnn.**n**. If that last number is there, you put it into the Internet address like this: first.last@**px**.fxxx.nxx.zx. Note the p before the additional number.

Note that the original order of the FIDONET numbers was reversed in the Internet address.

APPENDIX D
INTERESTING AND USEFUL WORLD WIDE WEB SITES

Welcome to Pat's List of Interesting (and sometimes useful) Internet Sites!

The Internet is a changing place, filled with an endless variety of utility and diversion. Here are a few of the thousands of Internet destinations that offer something for everyone. Note: A few of these sites may collide with the sensibilities or politics of some.

Keep in mind that, on occasion, site addresses may change or be too busy to respond. If you receive an error when you try to access a site, try again shortly. If the site address hasn't changed and the server is still operating, you'll eventually get through!

Ameritech World Wide Web Home, http://www.aads.net/

Andy Warhol Museum Home Page, http://fridge.antaire.com:80/warhol/

ANU Bioinformatics, http://life.anu.edu.au:80/

ANU Art History Exhibit, http://www.ncsa.uiuc.edu/SDG/Experimental/anu-art-history/home.html

Archie Request Form, http://hoohoo.ncsa.uiuc.edu/archie.html

AstraNet, http://www.astranet.com/home1.html

Avion Online Newspaper, http://avion.db.erau.edu

Banned Books On-line, http://www.cs.cmu.edu:8001/Web/People/spok/banned-books.html

Beginner's Guide to HTML, http://www.ncsa.uiuc.edu/demoweb/html-primer.html

Britannica Online, http://www.eb.com/

British Columbia, http://www.cs.ubc.ca/

BSDI Home Page, http://www.bsdi.com/

Campus Map, http://litwww.cwru.edu/CWRU/maps/main.html

Carnegie Mellon, http://www.cs.cmu.edu:8001/Web/FrontDoor.html

Census Information, gopher://bigcat.missouri.edu/11/reference/census/us/basictables/us.text/places

CERN Home Page, http://info.cern.ch/

CICA's WWW Server, http://www.cica.indiana.edu

City of Cambridge, Massachusetts — Homepage, http://www.ai.mit.edu/projects/iiip/Cambridge/homepage.html

Classified Advertising, http://www.imall.com/ads/ads.shtml

Commercial Sites on the Web, http://tns-www.lcs.mit.edu/commerce.html

Commercial Servers on the Web, http://tns-www.lcs.mit.edu/commerce/servers.html

Commercial Services On the Net, http://www.directory.net/

Commercial Use, http://pass.wayne.edu/business.html

CompUSA, http://comp-usa.mcs.net/

CompuServe's Web, http://www.compuserve.com

Computer Express!, http://cexpress.com:2700/

Cornell Law School, http://www.law.cornell.edu/lii.table.html

Cornell Theory Center, http://www.tc.cornell.edu:80/ctc.html

Cryptography, PGP, and Your Privacy, http://draco.centerline.com:8080/~franl/crypto.html

Currency Exchange, http://www.ora.com/cgi-bin/ora/currency

Current Weather Maps/Movies, http://clunix.cl.msu.edu:80/weather/

Data Sources By Service, http://info.cern.ch/hypertext/DataSources/ByAccess.html

Data Research Home Page, http://dranet.dra.com/

DESY Home Page, http://info.desy.de:80/

Doctor Fun, http://sunsite.unc.edu/Dave/drfun.html

Downtown Anywhere - Front Street, http://www.awa.com

ECE WWW Page, http://www.ece.uiuc.edu

Entertainment Technology Center Home Page, http://cwis.usc.edu/dept/etc/index.html

File Room Censorship Archive home page, http://fileroom.aaup.uic.edu/FileRoom/documents/homepage.html

Finger Gateway,http://cs.indiana.edu/finger/gateway

FTP Sites, http://hoohoo.ncsa.uiuc.edu:80/ftp-interface.html

Global Network Navigator Home Page, http://www.ora.com/gnn/GNNhome.html

GoldSite Europe, http://www.cityscape.co.uk

Gopher://una.hh.lib.umich.edu:70/00/inetdirsstacks/citizens:bachpfaff,gopher://una.hh.lib.umich.edu:70/00/inetdirsstacks/citizens:bachpfaff

Gopher Menu, gopher://gopher.ceweekly.wa.com:70

Gopher Menu, gopher://gopher.lib.ncsu.edu:70/11/library/stacks/Alex

Gopherspace Overview,

gopher://gopher.micro.umn.edu:70/11/Other%20Gopher%20and%20Information%20Servers

Grand Canyon National Park, http://www.kbt.com/gc/

Home Pages, http://www.homepages.com/

Honolulu Home Page, http://www.hcc.hawaii.edu/

HTML Quick Reference, http://www.ncsa.uiuc.edu/General/Internet/WWW/HTMLQuickRef.html

ICSI, http://www.icsi.net

Illinois Weather, http://www.atmos.uiuc.edu/wxworld/html/general.html

In Perspective Newsletter, http://www.wiltel.com/perspect/homepers.html

Index of /pub, ftp://ftp.csd.uwm.edu/pub

Indiana Home Page, http://cs.indiana.edu/home-page.html

Information By Subject, http://info.cern.ch/hypertext/DataSources/bySubject/Overview.html

InfoSeek Home Page, http://www.infoseek.com

Interleaf, Inc., http://www.ileaf.com/

Internet Movie Database at Cardiff UK, http://www.cm.cf.ac.uk:80/Movies/

Internet Talk Radio, http://www.ncsa.uiuc.edu/radio/radio.html

Internet RFCs, http://www.cis.ohio-state.edu:80/hypertext/information/rfc.html

Internet Web Text, http://www.rpi.edu/Internet/Guides/decemj/text.html

Internet Services List, http://slacvx.slac.stanford.edu:80/misc/internet-services.html

Internet Index, http://www.openmarket.com/info/internet-index/current.html

Internet Store, http://www.medium.com

InterNIC Info Source, gopher://is.internic.net:70/11/infosource

IntNet Online Home Page, http://www.intnet.net/

Job Search, http://www.umich.edu/~philray/job-guide/

Le WebLouvre, http://mistral.enst.fr/~pioch/louvre/

Library of Congress Vatican Exhibit,
http://www.ncsa.uiuc.edu/SDG/Experimental/vatican.exhibit/Vatican.exhibit.html

Live Access to Climate Data,http://ferret.wrc.noaa.gov/ferret/main-menu.html

Lysator ACS Sweden, http://www.lysator.liu.se:80/

Monster Board!, http://www.monster.com/

National Center for Atmospheric Research, http://http.ucar.edu/metapage.html

NCSA Home Page, http://www.ncsa.uiuc.edu/General/NCSAHome.html

NCSA Gopher, gopher://gopher.ncsa.uiuc.edu:70/1

NCSA Mosaic Starting Point,
http://www.ncsa.uiuc.edu/SDG/Software/Mosaic/StartingPoints/NetworkStartingPoints.html

NCSA Mosaic Demo Document, http://www.ncsa.uiuc.edu/demoweb/demo.html

NCSA Mosaic's 'What's New'Page,
http://www.ncsa.uiuc.edu/SDG/Software/Mosaic/Docs/whats-new.html

NCSA Access Magazine, http://www.ncsa.uiuc.edu/Pubs/access/accessDir.html

NCSA Mosaic Home Page,
http://www.ncsa.uiuc.edu/SDG/Software/Mosaic/NCSAMosaicHome.html

Net Happenings WAIS index, http://www.internic.net/htbin/search-net-happenings

Northwestern Home Page, http://www.acns.nwu.edu/

NPR Home Page, http://www.npr.org/

NSF Network News Home Page, http://www.internic.net/newsletter/

Ohio State Home Page, http://www.cis.ohio-state.edu:80/hypertext/information/information.html

Original (UMN) Gopher, gopher://gopher.micro.umn.edu:70/1

Pathfinder Home Page, http://www.timeinc.com/pathfinder/Welcome.html

Postmodern Culture, http://jefferson.village.virginia.edu/pmc/contents.all.html

PSC Gopher, gopher://gopher.psc.edu:70/1

Publicly Accessible Mailing Lists - Index by Name, http://www.NeoSoft.com:80/internet/paml/byname.html

Purdue Weather, http://thunder.atms.purdue.edu/

Purdue On-Line Writing Lab Web Server Home Page, http://owl.trc.purdue.edu/

San Francisco Free Press, http://www.ccnet.com/SF_Free_Press/welcome.html

SBA: Small Business Administration Home Page, http://www.sbaonline.sba.gov

SCO World Wide Web Home Page, http://www.sco.com

SCOOP! The CyberSpace Tip Sheet, http://www.clark.net/pub/journalism/scoop.html

SDSC Gopher, gopher://gopher.sdsc.edu:70/1

SDSU Sounds, gopher://athena.sdsu.edu:71/11/sounds

Shopping 2000, http://www.whopping2000.com/

Silicon Graphics' SILICON SURF Home Page, http://www.sgi.com

Solar System, http://seds.lpl.arizona.edu/nineplanets/nineplanets/nineplanets.html

Spider's Web, http://gagme.wwa.com/~boba/spider.html

SSC Home Page, http://www.ssc.gov/SSC.html

state51, http://www.state51.co.uk/state51/

UIUC Weather Machine, gopher://wx.atmos.uiuc.edu:70/1

UIUC Gopher, gopher://gopher.uiuc.edu:70/1

UNC-Chapel Hill home page, http://sunsite.unc.edu

UniPress W3's Will T. Bill, http://www.unipress.com/will-t-bill.html

University of Illinois at Urbana-Champaign, http://www.ncsa.uiuc.edu/General/UIUC/UIUCIntro/UofI_intro.html

U.S. Congress Info, http://thomas.loc.gov

Veronica Search, gopher://veronica.scs.unr.edu:70/11/veronica

Web Servers Directory, http://info.cern.ch/hypertext/DataSources/WWW/Servers.html

Web/Net T-Shirts, http://sashimi.wwa.com/~notime/mdd/www_shirt.html

Web Overview, http://info.cern.ch/hypertext/WWW/LineMode/Defaults/default.html

Web Project, http://info.cern.ch/hypertext/WWW/TheProject.html

Web News, http://info.cern.ch/hypertext/WWW/News/9305.html

WebCrawler, http://webcrawler.cs.washington.edu/WebCrawler/WebQuery.html

Weblint, http://www.unipress.com/web-lint/

Welcome to NetMarket!, http://www.netmarket.com/

Welcome to the Metaverse, http://metaverse.com

Welcome to Pizza Hut!, http://www.pizzahut.com/

Welcome to the White House, http://www.whitehouse.gov/

Welcome to ENTERTAINMENT WEEKLY, http://www.timeinc.com/ew/Welcome.html

Whois Gateway, gopher://sipb.mit.edu:70/1B%3aInternet%20whois%20servers

Windows Mosaic home page,
http://www.ncsa.uiuc.edu/SDG/Software/WinMosaic/HomePage.html

World Wide Yellow Pages, http://www.yellow.com/

Worldwide WWW Information, http://wings.buffalo.edu/world

Zippy The Pinhead, http://www.cis.ohio-state.edu:84/

APPENDIX E

GETTING ACCESS

In medium to large size cities, Internet access providers seem to be popping up with the same frequency as Radio Shack stores. In rural areas, far from even small cities, Internet access appears to be just a wish. In fact, obtaining Internet service is now quite prevalent no matter where you live.

If you're in a rural area, you may either dial long distance into a city, then pay a provider's access charges, or you may use national providers such as NetIowa or AlterNet, who charge less than the combined cost of long distance plus normal access charges for city-based providers. They are not cheap, but they do offer access. Reach NetIowa at 1-800-546-6587. Reach AlterNet at 1-800-488-6383. Your author has used both, and endorses them without hesitation.

If you're in a city of any size, there is probably someone with an Internet business. If a company such as Netcom doesn't have a local access number, an independent such as RCInet in Dayton, Ohio probably does. You can find Internet providers by one of several ways. Here's where to ask:

- A local university's computer department. They might offer a freenet.

- A local computer user group of some kind. These groups normally meet once a month, in the evenings, during the middle of the week.

- A local computer store.

- In the near future: Your telephone book's yellow pages.

- A local BBS.

Telephone service carriers such as MCI, Sprint, AT&T, and the regional "baby bell" companies such as Ameritech and Bell Atlantic now or will soon offer Internet services. Look for their ads in computer and online magazines or call them. The access charges from these companies are very reasonable.

Finally, there are the commercial online services such as America Online, Delphi, and CompuServe. Remember that these companies offer metered Internet access and have virtually no local phone number service to rural areas.

INDEX

175